MONEY IN THE
CHURCH

Into Our Third Century Series

MONEY IN THE CHURCH

JOE W. WALKER

Alan K. Waltz, Editor

ABINGDON   Nashville

MONEY IN THE CHURCH

Copyright © 1982
by the General Council on Ministries
of The United Methodist Church

Library of Congress Cataloging in Publication Data

WALKER, JOE W. (JOE WILLIAM), 1925–
    Money in the church.
    (Into our third century)
    1. Church finance. I. Title. II. Series.
BV770.W34   262'.076'0681   81-20583   AACR2

ISBN 0-687-27160-6 (pbk.)

MANUFACTURED BY THE PARTHENON PRESS AT
NASHVILLE, TENNESSEE, UNITED STATES OF AMERICA

Contents

Foreword

In 1984 The United Methodist Church will observe its 200th anniversary. The Christmas Conference of 1784 is most often regarded as the formal beginning of the Methodist movement in the United States. This historic meeting adopted the Articles of Religion, established a polity, elected Thomas Coke and Francis Asbury as superintendents, consecrated Asbury at the hands of Philip Otterbein and others, took other organizational steps, and called for a rebirth of evangelism and scriptural holiness in the new nation.

The observance of the bicentennial of The United Methodist Church is a time when we pause to reflect upon how the Wesleyan vision of holy love and vital piety spread throughout the nation. In the report of the Bicentennial Planning Committee, approved at the 1980 General Conference, we have these words: "As we approach the end of our second century, we look forward with excitement and hope to the beginning of a third century in the service of our Lord. Our concern is that, through our recognition of the past and our affirmation of the present, we will be called into the future as new beings, refreshed by our experience of Christ, revived in our commitments to bring salvation, peace, and justice to all of God's children, and renewed as a people of God in our own time."

The occasion of the bicentennial is a time to anticipate soberly the future and to assess ourselves carefully as we move into our third century. Our inheritance is one of great achievements. We have seen periods of great expansion in our denomination, and we are now experiencing a time of contraction and retrenchment. Yet the challenge and vision are still present—to serve in the name of Christ and to spread the call to salvation and spiritual rebirth. We need to experience anew the sense of mission and purpose that filled our predecessors with the power to evangelize a nation.

Again, we turn to the words of the report of the Bicentennial Planning Committee to the General Conference: "The future is a time for new birth and our Bicentennial prayer will be a call to a new birth of the fervent spirit of Methodism, to a new birth of personal obedience to the Christ, to a new birth of creative local congregations, to a new birth of evangelical zeal, and to a new birth of our vital commitment to peace and social justice."

You, as a United Methodist lay member or pastor, and your congregation have a significant role both in the celebration of and in the search for and the making possible of the new birth in our denomination. It is the people in the pews and pulpits of United Methodism who must reestablish our identity and purpose and infuse it with the excitement and commitment to bring its mission to fruition. We believe that, through the thorough examination of who we are as United Methodists, what we want to accomplish, and how we choose to pursue our goals, we will find the renewed purpose and vision to complete our task in the name of Christ.

Into Our Third Century, a series of books initiated by the General Council on Ministries with the encouragement of the Council of Bishops, is intended to assist your reflection on and discussion of the issues confronting The United Methodist Church. The books are based on individually commissioned studies and research projects. Over a four-year period, beginning in 1980, seventeen separate volumes are being released. The present book, *Money in the Church*, is the thirteenth in the series. Books already published are listed opposite the title page. Others scheduled for release deal with social movements and issues, outreach ministries, and polity. The last book will draw upon the insights gained in the series and focus upon the potential for The United Methodist Church in its third century. This concluding volume will be designed for use as a study book in local church classes, organizations, and discussion groups.

The General Council on Ministries is pleased to commend to you this book by Joe W. Walker. *Money in the Church* provides us with an insightful analysis of the ways in which money is promoted, received, and used in The United Methodist Church. Former patterns of giving are described as well as present ones. The motivations used in our promotional approaches are compared with the motivations members believe are important. We are helped to understand some of the financial pressures which the denomination will be facing in the years ahead and some of the ways by which these challenges can be met. The book deals with money, and yet more. It is concerned with the ways we think about and express our faith commitment as reflected by the financial choices each of us makes in response to the requests and appeals for the many programs of The United Methodist Church.

Explore with the author the issues raised. Share your reflections and reactions to this book with others in your congregation. Discuss it with district, conference, and general church leaders. Your responses will also be welcomed by the members and staff of the General Council on Ministries.

Norman E. Dewire
General Secretary
Alan K. Waltz
Editor

General Council on Ministries
601 West Riverview Avenue
Dayton, Ohio 45406
April, 1982

CHAPTER 1

Introduction

United Methodists long have had a love/hate relationship with money. They hate to talk about it, yet talk about it more than any other subject. There is a mystique surrounding money. It is considered highly materialistic but, at the same time, takes its place in most churches as the symbol of personal dedication. Ceremonially, it is placed on the altar to the singing of the Doxology. The offering takes its place along with fried chicken and warm hearts as the authentication that a gathering is truly United Methodist.

In its own way, money as an offering is the most tangible form of our community as the church. Giving it serves as the most obvious common act in which all participate. The use of money displays the most shared endeavor of the entire community of faith.

Money has been described as power that is portable, transferable, and storable. Every week collection plates are passed in more than 38,000 United Methodist churches in the United States, money is given, and the denomination is able to go about its business. Local church treasurers in country kitchens with pens and ledgers join hands with national treasurers, backed by accountants and computers, in transferring, storing, and passing on the power to where the work can be done.

Money in the church is almost always immediate and current. Little if any is given out of personal savings. Most comes directly from weekly paychecks in competition with

11

other immediate demands. In turn, the church, at all levels, exists on a hand-to-mouth basis. Few reserves are held by local churches, annual conferences, or national agencies. Except for the pension fund and a few designated reserves, the church operates financially from day to day.

On the average Sunday, 38,500 local church treasurers will receive almost $29 million. Seventy-nine cents of every dollar given will be used by the local church for all its internal and local needs. Sixteen cents will go to the annual conference for its programs and maintenance. Another five cents will go to the national agencies for everything from missions to magazines. Of the total, thirteen cents will go to what commonly is called benevolences—some local, some national, less than two cents of which go for work beyond our national boundaries.

Money, more than any other topic, occupies the agendas of local church administrative boards, annual conferences, and the General Conference itself. How much will it cost? and Where are we going to get the money? probably are the two most frequently asked questions in the church.

This book is about money. It is not a how-to on raising money, or a guide to keeping track of it, or a handbook of helpful hints on how to spend it. While faithful to facts, it is not an attempt to do a scientific study. It does attempt to test some ideas about the part money plays in The United Methodist Church.

I have been traveling the church this past year, interviewing individuals and holding dozens of meetings with laity and clergy about money. The previous ten years were spent as director of the Advance, with all the contacts that gave me. The Advance is the designated giving program for missions. What has been learned in the process is how little I really knew about money in the church.

The reader should not treat this book as the latest authority but rather as containing some ideas that are designed as much to elicit disagreement as they are to gain enthusiastic amens. The final goal of such a book is to bring the discussion of money in the church out into the light of day.

Some statistics are used in this book. I used several sources in attempting to find out who gave how much to what. Mergers of denominations, different bookkeeping methods, different fiscal years, and other variables make all these figures accurate only as general guides to illustrate the larger picture. If you find mistakes, I accept all blame. Where credit is due, please give it to the editors of *The Methodist Fact Book*, a handy volume that was published regularly in earlier days by the Council on World Service and Finance. Credit, as well, the numerous copies of the General Minutes and the helpful staff of the General Council on Finance and Administration, whose accurate figures always were accompanied by warm personal friendliness.

An apology is due for my continual references to the former Methodist Church and the seeming disregard of the Evangelical United Brethren history. From discussions with EUB friends, I got the general feeling that what I have said here about earlier Methodist practices would apply as well to the EUB tradition.

A word of gratitude to Ezra Earl Jones and Alan K. Waltz of the General Council on Ministries for their expertise and continuing personal support, to Jeanne Walker and Sherl Gonzales, who made typed sense out of my obscure handwriting, and to the congregation of Oregon's Lake Oswego United Methodist Church and my colleague pastor, Tom Tate, who told me they missed me while I was off researching, whether they really did or not.

One final note. I believe talking about money in the church is holy talk, deeply theological, and as sacred as prayer. I believe using money in the church is both terribly serious and lots of fun. The only thing more exciting than raising money for the Kingdom is spending it for the Kingdom!

CHAPTER 2

Early Days

There is a non-money strand of history in our church. This was especially true in rural areas, in small churches, and in the South following the Civil War. Money was a scarce commodity in most rural communities. Instead of using money, the barter system was the way goods and services were given and received. Goods were exchanged, labor shared, and food grown. The preacher was not the only one receiving chickens and corn in payment for services. So did the dentist and the lawyer.

With the parsonage came land for growing a garden, a barn for the cow, and an acre or two of good timber for wood. Occasional organized giving efforts called "poundings" brought in flour and wool and cotton. What little money was given was enough to keep the parsonage supplied with coal oil for light, with books, and with other store-bought necessities.

How, then, was money used, and where did it come from in these small rural southern churches? Different needs for money were met in different ways. Money was needed to pay the small stipend given to the preacher, to pay the "conference claims," and to buy those items used by the local church that could not otherwise be made, borrowed, or given, such as hymnbooks, pencils, Bibles, and coal oil.

The Preacher's Stipend

It was the stewards who, once each quarter, got the money together to pay the preacher. These venerable gentlemen took their job very seriously and made the rounds collecting, mostly from themselves. All too often the faithful thought the "quarterly steward's collection" meant precisely what it said, a quarter.

Bishop Roy Short tells about his own experience in the 1930s as a presiding elder in a rural district of Kentucky. "I remember that the first quarterly conference I ever held was on the weakest charge in the conference, the Wolf Creek Circuit. They had five churches, including a little old church called Mt. Hope. The stewards brought in the money. It was $12. This is all the preacher would have to live on for the next three months except for the food the people gave him. In those days, a percentage went to the presiding elder (as the district superintendent was called then). There was a question in the minutes, 'What has been raised for the support of the ministry and how has it been applied?' In our conference, 10 percent went to the presiding elder. This preacher said, 'Well, Brother Short, that's $1.20 for you and the rest for me!' I gave it back. I couldn't take it. I'd had a station church, a good church. This was during the thirties, the depression, and I'd been getting $3,200. I went to my next quarterly conference, and they had four churches. They brought in $36. The preacher said, 'That's $3.60 for you and the rest for me.' I shoved it back. I remember it was on my birthday. I had to ride a horse to get in to that church. I later learned that the man ahead of me scheduled the hardest churches first, trying to get in ahead of the fall rains. I went to one little town and got $35. I thought I'd struck oil."

Bishop Short pointed out that the size of salary was not always a true measure of how well a preacher lived. Because of the barter system, a pastor of a three-point country charge might live much better on $600 a year than the station preacher in the county seat who got $1,200 but little else.

Conference Claims

While the stewards collected to pay the preacher, the preacher had his own collecting to do. His job was to collect the conference claims. Then, as now, these claims went for such things as missions, Christian education, and for all work beyond the local church. The preacher went around to his members and literally begged for this money. In more than just a few places, it was necessary, just before annual conference, to have what they called an "annual tug," a mighty effort made to assure the preacher had enough to pay the conference claims.

Annual conference sessions came in the fall, a good time—the time when crops were harvested and money was most available. As the preachers rode in to this annual gathering, they knew they each would be asked two questions by the bishop. The first was, How many conversions have you had?; the second was, What about the conference claims? It was the pride of every preacher to be able to stand and answer the second question with, "Everything in full, Bishop!"

Small Offerings

The third way money was raised and used was with the offering. It never was very much, but most small rural churches did not need very much once the preacher was paid and the conference claims met. These offerings bought hymnals and coal oil and such other needs for the congregation. When some larger need came up that could not be met by giving labor or chattels, there were always rummage sales, quilting parties, cake walks, and bazaars.

There were certain values in this non-money way of doing the work of the church—values that we more moneyed folks may have lost. Services and goods given had a special touch that money cannot match. It well may be that the tenacious continuance of such things as bazaars and other money-making programs are much less the result of an unwillingness to give cash than they are a symptom of a need to make gifts more personal than money allows.

A layman in Georgia shared his memories. "Forty years ago there was no newsletter sent out, no printed program on Sunday morning, and no regular announcement about money except at the end of the year when the old presiding elder would come around and say, 'We got to get this much before the conference.'"

He went on to tell about the system used to support missionaries who, while on furlough, itinerated among the churches—a system we would consider paternalistic and degrading today. "When a missionary came to speak, he would then stand at the door, and the people would drop a dime or dollar into the plate." Why did people give in those days? "It was an emotional response, not a carefully thought-out response to the overseas work."

Meantime, in cities and towns and larger churches, money was more plentiful and played a larger role in what the church was all about. Regular offerings were received. Pledging and the use of envelopes appeared at least by the turn of the century. Other denominations used a variety of methods (such as pew rent, dues, and bingo) for assuring that money came in. Except in a few places, these methods were not used by our Methodist or EUB predecessors in the church.

Our heritage was one that stressed the voluntary nature of giving, although social and theological pressures were applied in more than a few places. Most people had some idea of what was expected of them. In case there were any doubts, the method of sermonically dangling them over the flames of hell (while not fully in keeping with our understanding of God's freely given grace) did get financial results!

Stewardship and Tithing

In the 1920s several things began to emphasize the importance of the members' giving money and the church's receiving it. In 1922, the Methodist Episcopal Church, South, organized the Board of the Laity and assigned it the major responsibility for church support. Such men as Bishop Cushman and George Morelock began to stress the concept of Christian stewardship. An emphasis on tithing became popular in the churches.

In the northern Methodist Episcopal Church the proviso for national and world programs grew under a fund called World Service. Annual conferences and the national church established promotional offices. The annual pledge became a regular part of the life of larger and more urban churches. The local church treasurer became a familiar officer. In northern Methodism there developed a system of having several local church treasurers—one for programs, one for missions, and possibly one for capital funds. The southern Methodist churches stuck to one local treasurer. A system was developed in the South at the annual conference level for the receipt of funds from the local church. In the North, the local churches sent money directly to the national offices in Chicago. These systems remained separate until the branches of Methodism united in 1939.

Centenary

The 1920s brought an emphasis on stewardship and tithing along with a more orderly system of handling money. It was also the time of the Centenary Movement, a huge crusade encompassing most branches of Methodism. The movement was designed to raise vast sums to reconstruct the church following the end of the First World War. Tremendous meetings were held around the country.

Bishop Lloyd Wicke remembers his father attending one such meeting, held in the Hippodrome in Cleveland. He returned from it deeply moved, literally weeping as he recounted to his family how speaker after speaker lifted up the vast needs for the reconstruction of churches and missions around the world. Bishop Wicke recalls how the size of his father's resulting pledge literally meant less food on the table for the family.

Vast sums were raised, but this great effort brought about two unfortunate results. Word got around that if this drive were successful it would end for all time the need for the church to raise such funds—an obviously unfulfilled dream. And, the church found itself administering vast amounts of money—a task for which it was ill prepared. Some good was done, but the program came apart at the seams as it tried to use the funds. It was a fiasco. No illegal or immoral acts were involved; the church just was not skilled or organized well enough to do the required task. The result was bitterness, disillusionment, and cynicism.

Then came the depression, a bitter blow to the church, just as it was beginning to move into a money economy in a major way. Offerings grew smaller as unemployment grew, banks failed, and the market plunged. Congregations hardest hit were those that had recently completed new capital improvements. Yet, as the years went on and the depression deepened, few churches were foreclosed. Banks settled for twenty-five cents on the dollar in some cases and extended payments in others. Evidence seems to be that local churches in that sad time had a better record for finally paying off debts and meeting regular bills than most secular businesses.

Gum Tree

Persons who remember those days give great credit to the stalwart pillars of the church—men and women who cared deeply about the church and its continued witness. One old gentleman in Alabama told me about the "gum-tree collection." When things really got bad and bills piled up, there would be a meeting of some of the churchmen under the gum tree out front. One had to earn one's way to a gum-tree meeting. Bills were discussed, and a collection finally taken; wallets were brought out, and precious dollars put in the hands of the eldest steward—and the church went on.

In the North and in the cities, it was a bit more sophisticated, but the system was the same. A notice was put in the bulletin, or an announcement was made in worship, The stewards will meet in the parlor after church. Everyone knew what that meant. Those faithful men would be making up the difference, and the bills would be paid. It was a high honor to be allowed under that gum tree or in that parlor, and costly too. But in thousands of churches—again and again in those depressing days—the church was kept alive.

While men gave money, women gave time. Pies were sold, quilts made, bazaars held, and the money forwarded to national offices for the maintenance of the Christian mission and ministries around the world.

To Summarize

The purpose of telling all this is not to recall a precise history but to share a bit of the feel of where we have come from. Sometimes as we work with our sophisticated systems that use computers and pledge cards, envelopes and apportionments, we need to keep in mind that we are not that far removed from less complicated days. They might have been less efficient, but they possibly were more human and humane. The question well may be whether we can learn to be as humane while we work more efficiently with money as we move into our third century.

CHAPTER 3

Donating Dimes and Dollars

United Methodism is big business. One corporation vice-president put it in his own terms. "Look at your outfit as I do," he commented, as we studied the latest General Minutes. "You have over 38,000 tax-free outlets largely paid for, with nine million steady customers—a third of them coming into the shop every week." I told him I was not too sure how steady those nine million customers are. He shrugged and went on, "In 1979 you grossed over $1.5 billion. That makes you one of the country's biggest businesses." He thought for a moment. "Only one thing. . . ." I waited. "How do you figure your profit?" Good question. Scripture came to mind, something about "What does it profit a person . . .?"

Money Dependence

In this day of double-digit inflation and deep concern over the economy, The United Methodist Church finds itself both part of and highly dependent on the economy. Our orientation to money leads us to believe it has always been so. Yet today the church, like all society, is financially interrelated with and dependent on the economy in ways that were not the case a hundred or even fifty years ago. Churches heated by pot-bellied wood stoves and lighted by kerosene lamps were not dependent to the same degree or in the same way we are in these days of electric power grids and imported oil. Members with their own gardens and wood lots and buggies were free in ways we are not today, as computerized bank balances and pension investment portfolios lock us into the rise and fall of the whole economic system.

Nineteen forty may have been a kind of turning point. Helped out of the Great Depression both by a New Deal and a new war, the economy began to shrug off its stagnation and people went back to work. In that year, The Methodist Church received a little under $76 million from its membership. That took care of everything—from paying the preacher to sending missionaries. That year the average member gave $10.26 to the church. A little over fifteen cents out of every dollar went to some form of benevolence. It is interesting to note that 77 percent of all benevolent giving came through three channels: World Service, conference benevolences, and the Women's Society of Christian Service. Only 23 percent came in through other kinds of benevolent giving. Later we will discuss how this changed during the next forty years.

The year 1940 might be characterized as the beginning of organized money in the denomination, as well as the economy. In earlier days it was used with a bit more slapdash and impulsiveness and with much less regulation, organization, and accountability. For example, the Church has funded missions ever since the day Paul suggested it might be a good thing to help the saints back in Jerusalem. But when that New Testament offering was received, it probably was not written into the local church's books, audited at the end of the year, and forwarded through a maze of institutional channels between Corinth and Jerusalem. Certainly Jerusalem was not required or equipped to send back an acknowledgment that the gift was received. Those were other days. Between then and now, many an offering has been received for the saints without benefit of ledgers or regulation. Missionaries once stood at the door literally hat in hand, taking to the mission field what was given them. Representatives of church institutions, hospitals, homes, colleges, and special projects itinerated through the connection raising funds, which may or may not have been recorded in some treasurer's books.

Handling money was more impulsive, haphazard, un-prioritized, and done with much less accountability. It also may have been more fun, more personal, and, in its own way, more successful. Having said this, however, no one advocates a return to such days. The very nature of today's society—with its Internal Revenue Service laws, require-ments for accountability, and sheer volume of money transactions—precludes such older ways. But there is a romantic yearning for a return to bygone practices. Efficient, properly prioritized, accountable funding systems seem to have about as much warmth as a sermon on management by objectives.

Methodical Methodists

No abrupt change could be noted in the early 1940s, but informality continued to give way to a system of priorities, channels, and accountability that conformed more to society's new money age.

A number of fascinating things happened between 1940 and 1980 in the use that the denomination made of money. We look first at several big movements of money in the church.

During the war years, very little church construction was done, as building materials became scarce and church structures rated a low priority in a controlled construction market. In 1944, only about 22 percent of the denomination's money was spent on building or debt retirement, with most of that going for debt retirement. Twelve years later, the church was at the height of a building boom, with thirty-six cents of every dollar going for some kind of capital funding of local churches—a dollar amount six times as much as in 1944.

Immediately after the war, there was a fantastic burst of energy in the area of benevolences. A quadrennial program called the Crusade for Christ and His Church gave a clarion call for reconstruction of churches all over the world. The membership responded in a magnificent way. Benevolent giving more than doubled in 1945 over 1944. Twenty-nine cents of every church dollar was going for some benevolent program. This increase was not made by cutting short other necessary programs, but by an infusion of additional money, resulting when an inspired program met the donors' needs to be involved in the needs of the world. This higher rate of benevolent giving continued in a measurable way for the next four years. It was not until 1949 that the church returned to the normal benevolence rate of about fifteen cents out of every dollar.

In 1944, about thirty-six cents of every dollar was being spent for ministerial services, including salaries, pensions, and other compensations for both local pastors and connectional officers. Four years later, this amount dropped to twenty-nine cents and in 1952 was down to a little over twenty-five cents. Actual salaries did not decrease. In fact, salaries continued to increase, but the proportion of the church's total financial resources going to clergy compensation did decrease. It remained at twenty-five cents until 1969. Then it began a gradual increase in the amount taken from each dollar until 1979, when 31 percent went for ministerial compensation.

Total income increased every year between 1940 and 1980. Drives for benevolent causes and needs for new church buildings, pensions, and other concerns meant that for a time one cause received more of the total dollars than another or more than it did in previous or following years. Usually these acute needs resulted in additional dollars going to that special cause rather than a shift of dollars away from other parts of the church. However, this was not always true, especially when church leadership seemed to work on the theory that there was only a limited number of dollars available. We will discuss that in detail later.

Benevolences

Year after year, the church gave around 15 percent of its total money to benevolences. Twice this pattern was broken significantly. The first was in 1945 and subsequent years when, as mentioned previously, the Crusade for Christ stimulated a magnificent response. The other change began after 1970. In that year, the church gave 16 percent of its money to benevolences. This amount then gradually began to decrease until 1979, when only 14 percent went to benevolences. That does not look like much of a change—only 2 percent, but consider what that meant in actual dollars. If in 1979 the church had given 16 percent as it did in 1970, there would have been over $32 million more for benevolent causes.

Shrinking Membership

In recent years, the church has given about 5 percent of its money to national programs, 16.5 percent for work within the annual conference, and 68.5 percent for local church programs. These percentages have been amazingly consistent since at least 1973 and possibly before that as well.

Another very consistent figure has been the per capita giving in terms of purchasing power. In 1967, the average member gave $64.40 to the church. In 1979, that figure increased to $154.77, just enough to stay ahead of inflation. However, the total purchasing power of the church fell during that same period for a very simple reason—it lost over 700,000 members, a loss of almost 7 percent. In 1979, it fell short by over $180 million of having the same purchasing power it would have enjoyed if the size of the membership had remained the same.

It should be noted here that studies have shown that the denomination did not *lose* members—it failed to gain new ones. The normal attrition due to deaths, transfers, and withdrawals did not increase over previous years. But the number of new members decreased. What may be an additional factor concerning money is that many of those who died were older and therefore may have been among the better givers. Since at least 1840, Methodists (and now United Methodists) have composed between 5 and 6 percent of the United States population. In 1980, this dropped to 4.28 percent—an unhappy trend that cannot help but have an impact on the church's income.

Another disturbing statistic is how United Methodists give compared to the rest of the religious community. According to the Princeton Religion Research Center, a total of $7.46 billion was contributed to religious organizations in the United States in 1967. Of that amount, 9.48 percent was given to The Methodist Church. By 1979, the total had risen to $20.14 billion, but only 7.37 percent was given to The United Methodist Church. This is a dramatic and startling change.

To Summarize

In the space of thirty-nine years, The United Methodist Church increased twentyfold the number of actual dollars it received and used. Millions of people put $22 billion in offering plates on more than 2,000 Sundays in over 38,000 different locations. This portable power, transferable treasure, storable strength has literally changed the shape of history, as it has been used in Christ's name next door and around the world.

CHAPTER 4

Getting It There

"You call that a system? It looks more like panic in a spaghetti factory!" He was a young accountant and had just examined the way United Methodists channel their funds from one place to another. After further study, he began to see some of the sense in it, but even then he wondered just how it ever got to be the way it is. "Is this the result of good procedure or pragmatic politics?" he asked. Someone suggested it probably was both.

Systems Develop

It was after World War II that most of the present-day system really came into its own. The Crusade for Christ and His Church, established in 1944, was dedicated to rebuilding a war-torn church. It doubled the giving to benevolent causes in one year and continued to upgrade mission giving in its quadrennial lifetime. The most well known program continuing from this movement is the Crusade Scholarship Program that has done so much to help educate persons for church leadership both abroad and among disadvantaged persons in this nation.

In 1948 came the Advance for Christ—another lively denominational program. This time it was the designated mission giving program called the Advance that lived on. It grew from a program through which a little over $1.3 million went into Christian mission during 1948 to one that conveyed over $21 million in 1980.

From at least 1948, there has been an intensified debate about fund-raising in each General Conference. When new programs are started at the national level, should they be funded by placing them in the World Service Fund, or should a new channel be started? By 1968, it was tacitly decided (and became something of an unwritten rule) that the World Service Fund could not bear any additional funding burden. If new programs were started, they would have to stand on their own with separate funds. By 1977, there were thirteen benevolence channels and three administrative funds in the denomination. In addition, the Advance program alone was then funding five distinct program areas. Thus, it could be said that there were twenty identifiable major funding channels for national programs and administration.

The inclusion in our consideration of the annual conference programs and, in some instances, district programs, further complicates matters. By the time the World Service request reached the local church, it was combined with the conference benevolences askings. The Advance program also included annual conference Advance Specials, which were mission programs within the bounds of the annual conference. The national administrative funds had their conference counterparts in Conference Ministerial Support and Administration Funds.

Some funds, such as the Fellowship of Suffering and Service, served their purpose and disappeared from the scene, but they have tended to be few and far between. Once started, most funds have remained. The Temporary General Aid Fund has lasted twelve years, somewhat less *temporary* than its name implies.

World Service

Meantime, in 1969 the basic fund of the denomination, the World Service Fund, stopped growing in its basic apportionment to the churches. In the 1968–72 quadrennium, $25 million was apportioned annually as the World Service Fund asking to the churches. In the next quadrennium, this was reduced to $23.5 million per year, and for 1977–80 it was $24,980,000 each year. Inflation required the national program agencies to use increasing amounts of their World Service dollars for administrative costs. More and more program funds became dependent on sources other than World Service.

Why was the World Service apportionment kept at approximately the same dollar level for twelve years? Two reasons have been offered for this decision. One national officer explained, "We have been through a period when supporters of various causes desired that support of these causes be given high visibility by having them stand on their own rather than included in the World Service Fund." The other reason given is that for a period of time in the 1960s the proportion of local churches paying 100 percent of their World Service apportionment diminished. It was thought that by maintaining the same apportionment for World Service, local churches would be encouraged to pay a larger percentage of it. This strategy proved to have only limited success. The unanswered question is whether the church would have tolerated new funds being added at the national level through the establishment of new funding channels and at the same time supported an increase in World Service. It seems so to this author.

Five Funding Systems

The denomination now seems to have established at least five clear giving systems for work beyond the local church, and it has arrived at an informal agreement as to their priority. The highest priority is Ministerial Support and Administration. It includes at the annual conference level such items as salary support for district superintendents, pensions, and other items related to personnel compensation. This fund carries the heaviest obligation for payment, the rationale being that the local pastor should not receive compensation unless pensions and salaries of the connectional clergy are paid as well. One eastern annual conference always refers to this fund as the Disciplinary Obligation—a name to prompt laity and clergy to pay in full.

A second implied priority of funding is World Service and conference benevolences—the combined basic benevolence funds for annual conference and national work. Until 1981, it had been allocated in some fair-share manner to each church as an asking, upon which each local church could take a formal vote of acceptance. The 1980 General Conference made the decision to apportion the fund but no longer asks for a vote of acceptance. This is a most interesting decision, which seems to come in spite of the growing desire of people in the local churches to be consulted and to make their own decisions. In any case, this fund carries with it all the weight of moral requirement. *The Book of Discipline* describes the World Service Fund as the "first benevolent responsibility of the Church."

The 1980 General Conference did increase the amount apportioned for the World Service Fund and did it in a new way—increasing it each year of the quadrennium rather than establishing it at a level that would continue for the entire four-year period. This gradual increase in the World Service apportionment was more than countered by requiring much more of it. The Mass Communications Fund and a part of the Temporary General Aid Fund as well as support of chaplains' activities, previously covered by a special offering, were all placed within the World Service Fund.

The apportioned amount for World Service is seen as a minimal need by the national church but usually is interpreted as a maximum goal by the local church. In its report to the 1980 General Conference, the General Council on Finance and Administration referred to the World Service apportionment to the conferences and local churches as a "base below which they will not fall." Some would question whether it even represents an adequate minimum. With general agencies receiving no more World Service dollars in 1980 than in 1968 and with costs having risen 109 percent, even payment in full of the total World Service Fund apportionment could not meet the needs of the agencies for the fulfillment of their programs and services. Nevertheless, most local churches feel they have achieved what was asked of them if they pay their World Service in full. Only a very few pay anything more.

A third manner of giving to programs beyond the local church is through what might be called apportioned askings. Like World Service, these funds are apportioned to annual conferences, which in turn apportion them to local churches on a fair-share pattern. Local churches are free to pay all, part, or none. There is not quite the priority given to paying these funds as is given the World Service Fund. Much less pressure is applied than that used to make good on "Disciplinary Obligations." Nevertheless, it is expected that local churches will participate in the Episcopal Fund, the General Administration Fund, Ministerial Education Fund, the Black College Fund, and other apportioned askings.

A fourth way of giving is through special day offerings. As the name implies, special days are assigned to causes, such as One Great Hour of Sharing and World Communion Sunday. These requests for funds are not apportioned to the local churches. Some local churches will not take the special offerings but will include them in the regular budget. Others will order the promotional material and envelopes and make a real effort to explain the purpose of each special offering to the congregation. It then becomes the individual member's decision whether to contribute or not. Special offerings depend very much on the popular appeal of the program being supported as well as the willingness of the pastor and other local decision makers to encourage the membership to contribute. More will be said about that later.

The fifth method for giving beyond the local church is the Advance program. This program presents options for giving to world, national, and conference progams of a missional and relief nature. Local congregations or individuals can pick any one or more of thousands of mission programs and projects. This program asserts that 100 percent of the gift will get to the actual project, as all administrative costs are borne by other funds. The Advance is highly voluntary except where specific projects are adopted by the annual conference, in which case pressure often is placed on local churches to witness to their conference loyalty by picking up their fair share. Bishops have been known to be very persuasive in getting support for Advance projects they have visited.

Except for one notable exception, the income from the Advance has gone only to three program divisions of the Board of Global Ministries. From time to time, other national agencies have eyed this attractive funding program, but as of this date all attempts to broaden the Advance to include work of other agencies have failed. The one exception was in 1976 when the General Conference asked the Advance to accept two Missional Priority projects with the General Council on Ministries as the recipient agency. This effort was not too successful as a fund-raising system. It seemed incongruous to some that a major portion of the priority programs would be placed in the second-mile funding channel.

These two Missional Priorities were not only funded through the Advance but depended on an apportioned Missional Priority fund as well. Dividing the funding into two channels was confusing and in the opinion of many counterproductive.

Other Possibilities

Pressures on national agencies for additional funds have given a nudge to what might well become a sixth level of giving through World Service Specials and through the establishment by the general agencies of foundations and other devices for the promotion and receipt of funds. World Service Specials has been a permissive channel for many years to accommodate gifts given to a national agency undesignated or directed toward one or more specific programs of the agency. It was tacitly understood that this channel would not be promoted. However, by 1980 national agencies saw the World Service dollar remaining constant and its purchasing power growing smaller. They either had to find new sources and channels of funds or cut out vital services. Leaflets began to appear encouraging the use of World Service Specials as a way to give to a specific board or program and still receive credit and remain loyal to the system. Through 1979, World Service Specials received such a small amount ($44,553, or .06 percent of total national level income) that it could hardly be considered a significant part of the funding system. It will be interesting to see if more aggressive promotion of World Service Specials by the three general program boards not eligible for the Advance will make a difference.

In March of 1981, a news article told about the organizing of a foundation by United Methodist Men. Another foundation in support of evangelism is at work. United Methodist Communications has a separate fund-raising enterprise to raise the $25 million in the 1981–84 quadrennium for the new Television Presence and Ministry fund. All of this may indicate that, while genuine need for funds can be enhanced by proper administrative procedures, these needs cannot be curtailed readily in a voluntary organization such as the church. Possibly a less conservative approach to the needed funds would somewhat curtail these more ad hoc funding systems.

United Methodist Women

One additional major national funding program needs to be considered. It is the funding provided to the Women's Division of the General Board of Global Ministries by local church units of United Methodist Women. Because of the unique constituency, these funds cannot be included in any priority ranking of national funding channels.

United Methodist Women has one of the most dynamic funding systems in the denomination and possibly in all of Christendom. With a membership of about 1.4 million in 1979, they sent over $13 per member to the Women's Division for work in Christian mission. This compares to the $7.56 per capita sent by the general membership of the church in 1979 for *all* other national work. Also during 1979, United Methodist Women provided almost $24 million for the mission work of their local churches and communities.

The largest portion of United Methodist Women's national funding comes through the undesignated channel called Pledge to Missions. Other channels are Call to Prayer, Supplementary Gifts, and bequests. A major effort is made to encourage undesignated giving through the Pledge to Missions. Supplementary Gifts is an available way to designate money for specific projects and programs, but it is not as actively promoted. Nevertheless, money given through Supplementary Gifts in 1979 had increased 143 percent over 1972.

During that same period, giving through the Pledge to Missions increased only 14.4 percent. The prevailing mood for more individual voice in deciding what to fund seems to have permeated even the local church United Methodist Women units. This is in spite of the Women's Division's insistence that undesignated giving is the better way to finance the church's mission.

Another interesting observation is that in 1972 over 53 percent of all funds given by United Methodist Women went to the Women's Division. By 1978, only 41.6 percent was sent. The rest was used locally in the church or community. This shift of priorities by local units to local programs meant a loss of over $4.5 million to the Women's Division for their programs.

Pensions

Payments for pensions for church employees, including clergy, have been included in the channel that goes to annual conferences commonly called Ministerial Support. However, the pension program is so large and is going through such a radical change that it deserves some special attention here.

Pensions is where the money is, and rightfully so. The General Board of Pensions managed an investment portfolio worth at least $850 million as of the first part of 1981. In 1980, it was the 108th largest corporate pension fund out of over 50,000 corporate pensions filed with the IRS. The board employs nine different investment firms as counselors who are given oversight by a highly skilled investment committee of board members as well as by the board staff.

Ask the average local church pastor or lay person, and they would identify the pension money their church pays as "part of all that stuff we pay the annual conference." Maybe so, but in fact this is a local church expense. The pension is a part of the deferred benefits that make up the pastor's compensation. If the local church were without a denomination, it would have to start a pension program of its own. It would be much more expensive and result in a much lower pension than handling it connectionally.

About 4.5 percent of every dollar put in the offering plate

goes for pensions. Most of this money eventually gets to the General Board of Pensions where it becomes a part of their large investment portfolio and thus benefits from careful management that assures the best returns from the invest-ment. Each annual conference sets its own pension rate and apportions the required amount of payment to each local church. Pensions are a local church necessity but enjoy the benefits of having the conference and national church involved.

Each month in 1980, the General Board of Pensions sent about 18,000 checks to widows, retired pastors, and dependents. Every month the dollars disbursed averaged about $5 million. That sounds like a lot of money, but the average monthly check came to only $277.78. The average minister serving thirty or forty years will receive only about $300 to $350 a month as a pension.

Pensions always have been a part of the Methodist tradition. In 1784 at the Christmas Conference, action was taken to provide relief for "worn out" pastors, funded by contributions from pastors themselves. Twenty Pennsylvania shillings were paid when they entered the ministry, and thereafter two dollars a year out of their yearly salary of sixty-four dollars. The recipients not only were required to be destitute, but to publicly confess that they were destitute.

In 1876, The Methodist Episcopal Church passed legisla-tion establishing the pension as an earned right, dependent on the number of years served. This was a move toward recognition that the pension is not charity but deferred compensation. In 1928, The Methodist Episcopal Church established the Ministers Reserve Pension Fund (MRPF), which utilized actuaries and other disciplines to establish a future-oriented reserve fund. It has served the denomination well for over fifty years.

In 1980, the General Conference approved a new Ministerial Pension Plan designed to phase out all unfunded liability (the term *unfunded liability* refers to the obligation to provide pension payments for years of service rendered not underwritten by sufficient funds to meet all of these future claims). Annual conferences have been anticipating the need to put pensions on a firmer financial foundation. In 1981, special fund drives for pensions have been or were being conducted by twenty-five conferences seeking over $103 million. To this effort is added the energy it now will take to bring the church into the new plan. While once pensions cost the church about 4.5 percent of its total revenue, this now will be increased to about 5.5 percent, according to the General Board of Pensions. The plan is that by the year 2022 there will be no more unfunded liability, and the cost of pensions then will be only 2.75 percent of the denomination's total annual income.

How will the church react to this increased obligation for the funding of pensions? Decisions were made at the 1981 annual conference sessions. The argument that pension funding has increased at a lower rate than either total church income or salaries was persuasive. The need to decrease or eliminate the unfunded liability was compelling. In some conferences, the limited dollars syndrome carried the day, and other programs have been curtailed or postponed to assure pensions its needed slice of the allegedly limited pie. In others, the more optimistic belief that people respond to proven need prevailed, and no other programs were held back.

A proviso in the new pension program allows a local church when permitted by the conference to pay the pension amount directly to the General Board of Pensions instead of to the conference. If adopted, this system would help local churches see the pension separate from conference funds and as the local deferred compensation it is.

There is no denying the reality that pensions are a financial priority of the denomination as it moves through the 1980s.

Whether funding this legitimate need is allowed to curtail or stop other aspects of ministry or mission has much more to do with attitude and optimism than it does with the ability of the membership to provide the funds.

Proliferating Channels

Did the church show wisdom in proliferating its channels instead of keeping everything in a few? Most would agree that if all the various funds had been kept in one fund, less money would have been given. There is an attractiveness in dividing the various causes into various funding channels. The question might be whether too many channels have been introduced.

Together Again

It is interesting to note that by the time all these various programs and their numerous channels reach the primary giver, the person in the pew, they usually no longer are divided into a multiplicity of channels. By then, everything may have been gathered up into a single item called the local church budget—at various levels, these numerous funding channels often were gathered together into a smaller number of askings in the hope they would be more understandable and acceptable by those at the next lower level.

We begin with General Conference, whose members decide that instead of every program agency being funded separately with a distinct funding channel for each, the requests will be put together in the World Service Fund. In its wisdom, the General Conference adds additional programs and funding channels only to the degree that it believes those at other levels will understand and accept them. These channels then go to the annual conferences. Here another gathering together takes place. For example, in several annual conferences there is a belief that too many funding channels would be confusing to members in local churches. Therefore, the conferences combine almost every asking into what they have named the Single Figure Fund or some other such compelling title. This approach is the extreme, but most annual conferences do some work on combining into fewer channels all the many funds and programs given to them by the General Conference. All these requests then reach the local church.

Whether it is Single Figure, Disciplinary Obligations, World Service, Advance, or whatever, the decision makers at the local level probably also will do some combining of their own. They may put everything in the program budget. They even may include the Advance and special day offerings in the single program budget to which their members are asked to subscribe.

This is a most interesting process. A multitude of channels are separately established by the denomination and are then put back together by the local church. One might wonder why they were divided in the first place. One reason well may be that there is a real need for a voluntary organization's funding methods to include a viable possibility of education and also provide participants the opportunity to choose.

By establishing a number of distinct funding channels, the General Conference is calling for information to be disseminated about each of the programs involved. It knows instinctively that if they were all put together this information would not be disseminated. Also, it is granting informal permission to the local churches to choose whether to fund each of these items. Through legal and political pressures, it sets up a hierarchy of priorities among the various funds, but allows a choice to be made at lower levels.

Then why do lower echelons of the church combine the funds? The hunch is that two things happen. First, there is a disregard for or an unawareness of the importance of information being shared about the programs. Unfortunately, the major pressure placed on local churches to pay is not by informing them but by using the motivations of duty and guilt—you have a duty to pay these, and you are guilty if you do not. The same motivations are at work in the local church as it motivates its members to give. Second, the annual conference may believe that a multitude of choices either confuses people or tempts them to pay some and not others. These are harsh judgments, but they are worth examining.

At a later time, we will look at the good and bad factors of having a number of channels for giving. We also will take a look at what really motivates people to give. For now, let it suffice to say that, in spite of the General Conference setting up at least twenty different channels for funding national programs and the annual conference adding many more of its own, by the time all this reaches the primary donor (the individual church member), all may be contained in one item called the Program Budget with no options except to subscribe or not subscribe.

It Works

So how are we doing? Does our funding system get results? The system seems to work well. The number and variety of channels do encourage information about programs to flow to the level where it is needed. There is enough selectivity allowed to make the system tolerable to a diverse voluntary organization. The decision-making process is diverse and widespread enough to make a fair claim to truly represent the broad spectrum of the membership. It is also diverse and widespread enough that when things go wrong it is extremely difficult to corner and blame someone. Possibly that quality might have saved us from the radical loss of funds suffered by other denominations over disagreements about some stands, programs, and attitudes at the national level. The powerful annual conferences also serve to some degree as buffers between the national agencies and the membership, being effective advocates of national programs and buffers against local ire.

The problems with the system have less to do with how it is organized than with the attitudes of some responsible for administering it. It well could be that the theory of only so many dollars to go around inhibited the denomination from raising World Service apportionments for a period of twelve years at the same time it was adding new channels for specific programs. The church probably would have responded to at least modest quadrennial increases in the World Service Fund.

The idea is that annual conferences could benefit from combining fewer of the various channels before forwarding them to the local churches. This strategy would encourage and require more information concerning what programs the funding channels are supporting. It would rely less on duty and guilt as motivations and more on understanding and acceptance by careful choice.

CHAPTER 5

Penny Pinching, Poor Mouthing, and Protesting

What stops people from giving? The evidence seems to indicate that personal motivation or lack of it influences giving patterns more than any other factor. The economic situation seems to have made little difference in the last forty years. The nation went through serious recessions in 1958 and again in 1974–75, but the total income of the church and its many programs continued without disruption.

That is not true for every local church or region. Serious layoffs and economic reverses can and do affect some local churches and entire regions, but as a whole The United Methodist Church has not been affected by the ups and downs of the marketplace. Even the combination of recession and continued inflation experienced as this study was being prepared was not impeding the continued dollar growth of church income.

Poor Mouthing

A Kansas wheat farmer described the seriousness of the 1980 summer drought and the impact it would have on his personal income. "Will you cut back on your giving to your church?" "Oh, no, I won't let that happen." "Will others cut back?" "No, the church would be okay." This seems to reflect, in general, the attitude found everywhere when financial reverses happen.

Much to the surprise of some clergy, the church is not the

first thing cut when there are financial reverses among the members. Poor mouthing is an old and honorable practice among the faithful, but they usually do not put their pocketbooks where their mouths are. As one Rio Grande Conference pastor commented, "If all you talk about is how poor you are, you don't know how poor you are."

Why is The United Methodist Church not hurt by recessions? It may be that most United Methodist members are in the stratum of society not too seriously affected by normal economic ups and downs. Most members are neither poor enough to be laid off nor rich enough to depend on clipping stock coupons for their incomes. They are that middle-income group that rides out the swings of the economy, neither benefiting from the ups nor being too badly hurt by the downs. However, it needs to be said that the nation has not experienced a true depression for forty years. In a depression or other massive economic dislocation, the church would surely be adversely affected.

Protest

Does protest affect income? Do people use the withholding of funds as a means of protesting things that happen in the church? Obviously they do. Every local church has experienced it when controversy appears. No one will deny that this happens. The more basic question is whether protest has a serious impact on the total income of the church. The answer seems to be that, while at certain times in some places it does, the general income of the total church has been changed very little by protest. At any given time, there are always a small number of persons who are angry, hurt, or otherwise disenchanted and no longer give. I daresay that has been a small factor ever since the day Paul took up the Corinthian offering for the saints in Jerusalem.

A belief that is very popular with some groups is that

church people vote with their feet and leave or stop contributing when they are displeased. Neither seems to happen. As stated earlier, studies indicate the loss of membership in the past decade has not been caused by an increase in the number of persons leaving but by a decrease in the number of persons joining. Neither persons leaving as a protest nor persons remaining but not giving has been significant in terms of the total income of the church.

It should be noted that while some people do register their opinions with their money, it is seldom to the extent of withholding. Usually, they redirect their funds toward other channels provided by the church. One person in New Jersey belonged to a church that seldom paid its World Service asking. Being devoted to the ministries provided through this fund, the member withheld his pledge from the local church and instead sent it to the conference treasurer—designated for World Service *to the credit* of the local church.

Back in the 1960s, a number of local churches in parts of the Southeastern Jurisdiction refused to pay the World Service apportionment as a protest against the denomination's strong stand on racism. However, the total income of most of these local churches remained strong. Except in rare moments, it seems that this redirecting of funds is a continuing phenomenon by which a few persons in the church express their convictions. The United Methodist Church as a total denomination has not suffered any significant withholding of funds from its total program because of disagreements or protest.

That is not to say that withholding funds never will be a factor in The United Methodist Church. It has been used in devastating ways in other denominations. Possibly one saving factor is an organization that spreads both authority and responsibility widely throughout the denomination. Blame may be placed on some segments of the church, but seldom is the entire denomination held to be at fault. Also, there is

more operational loyalty and trust among the members than
seems apparent during a time when relatively small vocal
groups are letting their disagreements be known.

Competition

How much United Methodist money goes to other
charitable or religious programs or agencies? There seems no
real way to measure this, but the feeling across the church is
that there is a large amount that goes in such directions. That
is a far cry from any kind of negative protest. In fact, most
clergy encourage their people to be involved financially in
community and national programs beyond the denomination. "Take all the United Methodists out of our United
Way," brags a layman in Virginia, "and there wouldn't be
much of it left."

United Methodism has been well known through the years
for encouraging its members to give time, talent, and money
in support of worthwhile causes. It is quite natural for the
members not to draw a distinct line in their giving. They not
only will give to United Way, the American Cancer Society,
Boy Scouts of America, and other causes, but they will give to
organizations that have programs similar in intent to those of
the denomination. Child "adoption" agencies (such as
Christian Children's fund), local private colleges of other or
no denominational affiliation, and even the preachers in the
electronic church all are recipients of the benevolence money
of United Methodist members.

There is a strong tendency on the part of clergy and other
leaders to object to such benevolent giving when it is directed
to agencies and programs that appear to be in competition
with the denomination. Two things sometimes are forgotten.
First, not too significant an amount of money goes to such
competing groups when measured against the $1.5 billion
that are given to the denomination. Second, the plaints of

pastors and other church leaders cause very little change in the giving patterns of the persons involved. Time and money might well be spent better in extolling the values of our own systems.

The church should give attention to disagreements and protest, but the attention never should be motivated by fear of losing funds. It should come out of a genuine concern for individuals. Also, if we are a diverse denomination, in fact as well as rhetoric, then disagreement and protest are healthy signs of the dynamic tension that might result in new insight and creativity.

This writer has observed three reactions of the church to disagreements and protest, reactions that might speak more to our paranoia than to our acceptance of diversity. First, the denomination's officials often overreact. Charges are made by some individual or group, and the church reacts by mailing a defensive response to every pastor most of whom either never heard the original charge or do not consider it to be all that important. Second, the church sometimes makes slight inferences that the critics may not be totally Christian. It is implied that those under attack are obviously prophetic as proven by the very fact that they are being attacked. Third, and possibly most ineffective, the church's response may imply that the critics are being picky since the things they object to only cost about four cents a member or some such small amount. This defense ignores the main reason behind the criticism, which has nothing to do with the volume of money but objects to the nature of the program with which they disagree.

The manner in which officialdom, from the local pastor to national agencies, responds to criticism is deeply related to the whole question of money. If protest and criticism do eventually lead to withholding or redirecting funds, it is seldom because of disagreement over actions or statements.

Instead it results when people believe that they are not being heard or that they are being rejected as persons of worth and dignity. Anger and arrogance usually have been evident on both sides of controversy. What is needed is a willingness for all parties to engage in a common search for truth as they accept their points of disagreement.

Dodging Issues

At times, money becomes a way of dodging larger issues. It is much easier to discuss the cost of a program than it is to discuss its value. In 1976, a study group presented the church with a thoughful document concerning the ethnic minority local churches in United Methodism that recommended making this issue a priority for the new quadrennium. As the paper made its way through various channels toward General Conference, it seemed never to be seriously discussed except to decide how much it would cost and how the money should be raised. The debate in General Conference itself was limited largely to these two questions. The issues that centered in the values of a racially and ethnically diverse fellowship and how those values could be enhanced and exalted never seemed to be seriously considered. The resulting failure to raise any significant amount of funds could have been predicted given the unwillingness to face up to the deeper issue.

Yet, at other times money becomes the way by which the church puts tangible witness and action behind what otherwise remains subjective and vague. Money requires a put-up or shut-up confrontation. Where an issue has been honestly faced and openly debated, the church then has put words and concepts into action through putting its money where its words have taken it.

Money always has played a role in the Christian fellowship.

Paul talked about taking up a collection for the saints in Jerusalem. John Wesley counseled his Methodists to make money, save it, and give it away.

The saints from then until now have been in the same paradox as the contemporary church—wishing there were more money and, at the same time, wishing it would go away!

Smallness Hurts

One area of discontent is in the small membership churches. A North Carolina pastor commented. "I am surprised at the loyalty the small churches give to their apportionments. They aren't getting a whole lot out of it." He explained that materials seem to be designed for the larger, better equipped congregations. There is a feeling that the small churches receive the most inexperienced or the least qualified clergy. A Kansas superintendent described what he called the survival syndrome in the small rural churches. "The church becomes so concerned with its own survival that it becomes a sickness. It feeds on itself. They tighten down and become more concerned about the roof than missions. You've got to break that syndrome."

The reality is that in small churches local costs, salaries, and utilities make up a larger percentage of total costs than in larger churches and are becoming more expensive. There is a general feeling that the smaller congregations are required to carry disproportionate shares of all apportionments. In spite of all this, the feeling is that per capita giving is greater in small membership churches than in larger ones. However, the general feelings of alienation, neglect, and unfairness must be addressed, or they could become a major problem in the area of finances and in other facets of the denomination's life as well.

Federal Cutbacks

There is a major way in which money within the denomination may be influenced by the nation's economic situation. It has to do with programs that are recipients of grants, loans, and other economic benefits from various levels of government. The withdrawal of funds from social services by the Reagan administration may drastically reduce the church's programs related to the welfare of persons. In some instances, these public funds have accounted for half or more of the monies spent. Health and welfare ministries, community centers, and aid for relief and development in other countries are all being threatened by reduction of federal funds. The denomination may have to consider a greater investment of its own money in such programs in order to avoid a total withdrawal of such services from people in need. The church may need to challenge the private sector to replace the withdrawn finances by supplying money through grants and other funds. More on that later.

The Loan Market

Another factor related to the public economy has to do with the availability of loans for capital improvement and growth. It is doubtful that the church could experience the dramatic growth of new churches in today's money market (high interest rates, down payment requirements, and the cost of land and materials) that it experienced in the 1950s. Money available for capital projects within the denomination itself has almost disappeared. Annual conferences, the National Division of the Board of Global Ministries, and the United Methodist Development Fund—all previously capable of providing a significant amount of the needed capital—now all report relatively little money available for building at a time when costs have risen. In the past, special drives in the annual conferences have provided money for church extension. It appears that in the next decade the seeming pressing need to have such drives for pension funds may make church extension funds difficult to raise.

Litigation

Another way in which the public affects the church is through litigation. Even when cases are settled out of court, as with Pacific Homes in California, the cost for legal counsel is in the millions of dollars. That settlement, itself, will cost $21 million in immediate loans. Similar situations have absorbed the church's time and money in other places in the nation. The rush to litigation is so severe that a type of malpractice insurance for clergy now is offered.

Taxes

Another aspect of the public economy that affects money in the church is an increasing pressure to tax some or all properties of the church. In some instances, local churches are paying a voluntary usage fee to compensate for community fire and police protection. This payment, whether voluntary or tax, could mean an added burden on the income of the church.

New Internal Revenue Service regulations have changed the reporting and deductions for individuals' charitable giving. This should not affect church income. The general feeling in the church is that not too much money is given to the church in order to realize a tax break. Some of the top denominational finance officers and many conference and local treasurers feel this will not have any significant impact on income.

Disposable income is described as the income people have left after taxes. The continued inflation has driven people into higher and higher tax brackets, resulting in less and less disposable income. There is what is called discretionary income—income not already committed to house payments, insurance, and other set and contracted costs. Economists say this kind of income also is decreasing in the average household.

How do decreased disposable and discretionary incomes affect the church's income? We can look at the past. Both disposable and discretionary incomes have decreased in the past decade, yet the average gift in the denomination by the average church member has grown not only in actual dollars but in purchasing power. It may be that we do not credit our people with enough faith to keep their gift to the church among their highest priorities. Even though the church may not be their first priority, it is not their last.

Increased Costs

Energy shortages, inflation, recessions, and other economic factors seem not to have reduced significantly church income, but they have made running the church at every level a more costly affair. As discussed earlier, capital improvements might not come at all easy in the near future. Local churches are spending more of their income for heating and lights. National officers find travel and meetings becoming prohibitively expensive. Even though total income may not be affected by the economy, the manner in which that income is spent may be dramatically affected.

To Summarize

This chapter by itself would be gloomy going. There are factors that cut down on income and others that make it more difficult to get the church's work done. Nevertheless, the income of the church has continued and should continue to be strong. If a depression or other major social or economic upheaval takes place, then there might be a significant impact on the denomination. Meantime, the members seem to give the church a higher financial priority than some give them credit. Factors are causing reprioritizing and rearrangement of budgets, but at this date they have not eliminated essential ministries. The factors that limit or rearrange national and world economics seem not as important in determining the local church's and the denomination's incomes as is the member's personal desire to give.

CHAPTER 6

Whom Do You Trust?

People give more as a result of from how they *feel* than from what they think. For that reason any discussion of giving must consider the whole matter of how we feel about each other in the church. Except for our fundamental relationship to Christ, nothing in the church is as vital as the feelings we have about each other—feelings that encompass faith, trust, acceptance, respect, and love or the lack of them.

For the past several years, there has been a dis-ease concerning our feelings about each other. This awareness of something being wrong has created a belief that we could solve things by restructuring or by offering different varieties of programs and priorities. But these restructured and varied program emphases, valuable in their own right, have not solved the problem. In traveling throughout the denomination for this study, it appeared again and again that the cause of the discontent had little to do with structure or the degree of concord concerning our actions or words. It centered around how we feel about each other.

Voluntary

The church is voluntary. It is the body of Christ. The church at every level is made up of people who freely choose to be a part of it. Even the sense of duty to grandma who lives down the street is disappearing in an increasingly transient society. Social pressure from neighbors and friends is diminishing as it becomes socially acceptable not to have close ties to the church. Those who are part of the church have exercised a very real option—they have volunteered. Duty and obligation are being replaced by free choice and love.

A voluntary act in this organization is giving money. It is a private act. Miss worship and everyone knows, but fail to give money to the church, and no one will know except a few finance people who have a tendency not to tell it around, even to the pastor. True, some people stop giving or give only a little as some kind of statement which they announce to everyone, but others just quietly and privately give very little or not at all, and few persons are the wiser.

In this most voluntary of all institutions, the most vital element seems to be our relationships to each other. To use Paul's symbolism, What does the hand think of the foot or the elbow, the eye? From usher to bishop, chancel choir to general board, this factor appears to be the single most important element in how we function as a church. This is as it should be, if the gospel is as incarnational as we claim it to be.

National Distrust

Complicating this situation is the general era in which we live. It is a highly suspicious and distrustful period in human history, especially within our own country. The Vietnam tragedy did have the positive effect of teaching us that presidents and others in high office may not know best what is good for the people. We developed a healthy distrust for judgments in high places. What we did not expect was that this distrust of government would spill over into other areas of life.

In the 1960s, the attitude often expressed was, "Don't trust anyone over thirty years old." Now as we are plunging into the 1980s, it has changed to, "Don't trust anyone over thirty miles away." I want us to examine this attitude because I have an idea it has influenced the way we use money in the church.

There is a growing tendency on the part of local church people to trust their own opinions, attitudes, and experiences. Compared to a hundred or even fifty years ago, they have good reason to have such trust. The days when they lived confined in their own narrow valley or hamlet largely is gone. Exposure to education, travel, literature, television, other cultures, and other means of experiencing life have given us all a broader understanding of the world in which we live. Across the denomination there are numerous local churches that have within their membership and community, persons who have had a wide range of experience and education in a scope that would not have been true several years ago.

In previous times, the local church was dependent on the general agencies, their representatives, and on the bishops to bring them the perceptions they needed about the world and Christian ministries. That is no longer the only source or even the most important source where such learning and opportunities can be found.

Self-Determinism

Something else has happened at the local level. It, too, has participated in what could well be called the primary revolution of the twentieth century—the discovery by the world's people of their own sense of self worth and the resulting practice of self-determinism.

It is remarkable that this revolutionary change could be

seen as happening around the world, but some persons cannot see it happening within their local churches. Some persons can applaud this revolution of self-determinism happening in other lands and in the disadvantaged portions of our own nation and yet have difficulty recognizing the value of it happening in local churches.

Well, it is happening, and it is having a profound influence on the relationships that exist within our connectional denomination. Local churches are practicing an involvement in those things that are important to them and are moving quietly away from involvement in things they are not convinced are important.

This self-determinism has not meant, necessarily, a nonglobal localism or parochial practice of the Christian faith. Because of access to information and experience by persons within their own congregations and communities, many local churches have a highly mature understanding of Christian ministry and mission. They want involvement in significant ministries. They continue to want positive channels of involvement in Christian mission. But members in local churches no longer desire to be involved with institutions that they perceive as condescending to local congregations. They are no more willing to be paternalized than are the overseas churches or other emerging peoples. If they have lost a sense of trust in the larger church, it is not so much because agencies or leaders are saying or doing things that disturb the local church, but because the *attitude* of agencies or leaders is perceived as arrogant and paternalistic.

The demand for fiscal accountability seems not so much a fear that money is being used in some unlawful manner as it is a means by which the local churches are requiring agencies to develop closer relationships with the total membership. As one annual conference leader commented,

"The bureaucracy lacks confidence in the membership. It does not believe that local-church level United Methodists can make good decisions."

Distrust of the Local Church

Now, let's look at the other side of this relationship, at the institutions beyond the local church. They seem not to understand the involvement of local United Methodist churches in the universal discovery of a sense of self-worth and their subsequent move to self-determinism. If institutions do feel the effects of the move to local self-determinism, they tend to perceive it as a move away from prophetic ministries and global involvement.

In talking with some national executives, there is a feeling among them that others on the national level believe their agency is in mission *in spite of* the local church. True, such persons are not the majority on any staff, but their numbers are large enough to have the attitude perceived at local levels. I believe that long service in a general agency tends to give one a "remnant" syndrome—a feeling that "we and we alone know and practice the true faith."

I can remember a general agency staff person talking to a group of us responsible for interpreting mission to the local churches. She was describing the need to identify with the poor. Finally, with a sigh, she stopped and said it really did not do any good to share with us because "those churches where you will speak are too caught up in the oppressive system to ever identify with the poor." Such attitudes are picked up quickly by the local membership and are resented deeply.

Some other persons serving institutions and agencies beyond the local church have an attitude that they are in mission or ministry *on behalf* of local churches. While this is a quantum leap forward from the "in spite of" attitude, it still appears as a paternalism that is unacceptable to the liberated people inhabiting the local churches today. Woe to the local pastor who tells the members that he or she is out doing Christian things on their behalf. Congregations are quick to inform such pastors that they, as laity, are capable of such good acts. They welcome the pastor to join with them in ministry but not to do it for them.

What local churches are asking of the church beyond their walls is for a genuine team concept to be established in which all members have a mutual respect and need for each other. Local churches do not want to give their money in order that some agency can be in mission but in order that they too can be in mission *with* the agency. There is a feeling of wanting to participate in a general atmosphere of mutual respect and need. The day of hierarchal structure has diminished in terms of authority. It needs now to diminish in the areas of education, works, and decision-making. Local churches want the church beyond their walls to be faithful to prophetic Christian ministry and mission, but that relationship now must become dialogical and not a one-way monologue.

To Summarize

Something *is* wrong, but it is not structure. Nor is it essentially a massive disagreement as to what is Christian mission or ministry. What is wrong is the way in which parts of the same church look at each other. On the one hand, local churches fail to understand how much they need the church beyond themselves both to understand and to practice the faith. On the other hand, many of the persons who work beyond the local-church level need to stop believing that they are the only ones capable of understanding or practicing the faith. They need to understand that the basic anger they experience from the local church is not because of what they do or say but because of the arrogant attitude with which they do it or say it. Both parts of the body need to develop a respect and a need for what the other has to offer and then to proceed *with* the other into doing and being what the church is meant to do and be.

CHAPTER 7

Gatekeepers or Goal-Setters

"Our pastor never talks to us about money," complained a woman in Kansas.

"They told me when I first arrived that I was to take care of the spiritual things," said a clergywoman in Tennessee, "and they would take care of the money."

In Mississippi, a church once paid no World Service or other apportionments and was struggling to meet its local needs. The members shared how a pastor turned things around. "The reason this church is giving so much compared to five years ago is because we have a leader who showed us how to give, so we give," explained the lay leader. A member added, "He gave us a whole new set of values called the kingdom of God. To give and do things in the church is a pleasure, where once it might have been a chore."

How well do pastors handle the matter of money in the church? Possibly no question raised more emotion than this one when discussed in the research for this study. There is a feeling that many pastors do not do an adequate job of dealing with money in the local church. This shortcoming is not just a lack of technical skills but has to do with a whole range of attitudes and feelings.

Still the Leader

The pastor is still the leader in the congregation. There is a strong feeling of trust in and reliance on the pastor so that his or her relationship to the question of money becomes very important. One black layman commented, "Where they trust the pastor, they will trust the system." In the Rio Grande Conference, a layman stated that trust in the local pastor was the single most cohesive factor in the life of local congregations.

"We're the key," agreed a group of pastors in Atlanta. "Trust or distrust of the pastor sets the tone for how the whole church is trusted." This group went on to say, "We carry the banner. We can claim the glory if we succeed and unfortunately have to take the blame if we fail." More than one layperson shared the feeling that the main motivation for paying apportionments was "to keep the pastor from getting in trouble."

Measured by Payments

According to numbers of pastors, one of the ways their skills are measured is by how well their church pays its askings and apportionments beyond the local church. Younger pastors resent this situation more than older ones. "There are other things we do that say more about how well we are doing," was the comment of a young New York pastor. Be that as it may, there seems to be general agreement throughout the denomination that local church support of annual conference and general church ministries is related directly to the pastor's involvement in providing information and stimulating motivation in the congregation. This expectation is stronger with conference and national leaders than with local church pastors or laity. Possibly this is because at local levels there is a recognition of the increasing part laity play in this task.

Also, other values are more readily seen against which the pastor can be measured. A pastor in New Hampshire defended his role by stating, "The old days where the pastor was the most intelligent person concerning giving of funds are gone. People are studying just where the money is going very carefully." But a conference officer in Oregon says, "The journals of three different annual conferences of which I have been a part show that there are certain ministers who have difficulty in paying their apportionments in every church in which they are appointed, and others who always pay them, even when appointed to churches which previously have had difficulty in paying them."

Attitudes

Do clergy have views about money in the church that are radically different from the laity? "I don't think so," replied a professional who has spent a lifetime raising money in churches. "They range from one to ten in their understanding, abilities, and attitudes regarding money—the same as do the laity. But a church can survive some laity with little skills or with negative attitudes regarding money. They cannot survive a pastor who is that way."

The general feeling across the denomination is that many clergy are not equipped to handle the subject of money in the church. This inability has to do not only with their skills but with their attitudes as well. Obviously this cannot be a statement that applies to all pastors. However, generally speaking it seems that pastors are perceived to be less prepared to deal with money matters in the church than they are with many other parts of their work. As a whole, pastors too feel this to be true, though not all agree to the extent of laity and church officers.

Why is this? A Kansas layman declares, "Our pastor never talks to us about money." In Georgia, a woman says, "Many pastors never preach on this subject, refuse to assist in a financial solicitation, and don't want to know anything about what a person gives. Pastors need to be educated to be bold in this regard."

Seminary Training

Most commonly heard is the complaint that clergy are not trained in matters dealing with stewardship or money. One national officer who works with funding charged, "The seminaries not only do not teach fund-raising techniques but do not set the biblical or theological basis for a Christian understanding of money. Because they see money in the church as an institutional necessity rather than a theological imperative and opportunity, their whole attitude and approach is counterproductive."

"Seminaries are void of stewardship training," complained a Mississippi layman. He would get an argument from some seminaries but not from others. "In 1978 in our seminary, 70 percent of our faculty worked together with a neighboring annual conference to articulate a theology of stewardship," commented one professor. A seminary president pointed out that the seminary was cooperating with the Stewardship Commission of the National Council of Churches to begin the Ecumenical Center for Stewardship Studies. Another rather wistfully commented, "This is one of about fifty issues we receive letters about from the church as to what we should do in the three years we have people studying in seminary."

While not in complete accord, the seminaries, when asked, mostly agree that by the time a student graduates he or she is not well prepared either in the area of stewardship or in the practical matters dealing with money in the church. One comment was that most students in seminary to not have a mind set that prepares them to relate to such matters. "Many students do not perceive the import of a concern such as stewardship until they are faced with the realities of parish practice," was the response of one seminary dean.

Three suggestions were made by seminary people to implement teaching stewardship and money matters in seminaries. One was to emphasize it during any intern experience provided students. The second was to encourage annual conference Boards of Ordained Ministry to assure that new clergy had some kind of experience in this subject during the two years served as preparatory for full membership. The third suggestion was that greater emphasis be given these topics in the continuing education programs being urged for all pastors. These all have merit. Seminary leaders generally are willing to concede that more emphasis needs to be given in the theological schools to this aspect of parish life. However, they do not believe the seminaries are equipped to do the whole job. Pastors also can be helped in other facets of their preparation as well as in their continuing education.

Salary and Pride

If pastors are not dealing adequately with money in the church, neither the entire fault nor the entire cure can be found in their training. Many other factors are involved.

"In my little churches, 60 percent of our budget goes for my salary," lamented one pastor in North Carolina. "If I get involved, it seems to me they think I am out to get money for myself." A pastor in Maine agreed, "I don't want to be accused of trying to raise my own salary." It could be argued that other professionals—doctors, lawyers, counselors—are in the same situation. Yet there is something so very personal about the task of the minister that it easily can be seen why there would be some reluctance by pastors to become involved in raising funds that are used largely for their own support, especially in smaller, less institutionalized, more personal parishes.

Another aspect is pride. "God didn't call me to be a beggar!" stated a pastor in Texas. "They never let me forget that part of what is raised buys my groceries and provides a house," said an Oregon pastor. The subtle but very real paternalism of some lay persons makes some pastors defensive. One of the best recourses to this is not to get involved in raising the funds. "I have no trouble approaching my people for missions," commented a California pastor, "but I sure hate to ask them for my own salary."

Conspicuous Failure

Money is very objective. It is conspicuous. Success and failure in this aspect of the local church's life is easily measured compared to more subjective factors such as spiritual life, love, and pastoral care. Sooner or later a church fails to meet its apportionments or even to raise its expected program buget. A few such experiences discourage some pastors from getting too involved again. They are inclined to say, Let the lay people do it! That way successes for the pastor can be assessed by other means, and this very measurable activity becomes less threatening.

Given the appointment system that tends to delegate the allegedly less-skilled clergy to the smaller, more difficult churches, is it any wonder that many clergy defend themselves by opting out of such a conspicuous failure-laden enterprise as fundraising? As one national promotion officer observes, "Survival, not mission, is their agenda."

Another aspect has to to with pastoral concern for the flock. In more than one congregation, the pastor finds the widows and hardscrabble farmers barely surviving financially. Along comes the denomination with apportionments, special days, and askings. The pastor views these as threats to his people and stands between the threat and the folks, as a good pastor should. This may be a misreading of both the people and of the requests of the denomination, but the pastoral love displayed has to be admired and surely should be understood.

One Oregon pastor made an interesting comment, "My bishop gave me two orders when he sent me here: Preach the gospel and preserve the institution!" He went on to say that the second order may not have been stated, but it was implied. The job evaluation of that pastor might be weighted more toward how well the institution was preserved than how well the gospel was preached. The whole conversation had centered around his reluctance to push a certain fund important to his superiors.

It reminded this author of how much easier it is to be prophetic at denominational or annual-conference levels than it is in the local church. It requires very little personal risk to take prophetic stands in those situations where one does not live with, marry, bury, preach to, and collect funds directly from the folks. All too often the failure of a pastor to take the same bold stand as do more distant leaders may seem to the latter as an abdication of the gospel, a personal cowardliness. What it may be is a very real need to be faithful to that second order that is always implied in a pastoral appointment, Preserve the institution.

On the other hand, the pastor may be misreading the congregation. They may be better prepared to deal with controversy and prophetic ministry than the pastor understands. "The church can absorb an awful lot of truth," said an experienced Tennessee conference officer. What is important here as we talk about money is to understand that some pastors do in fact protect their congregations from conference and national action out of a keen desire to make sure the church keeps going. Faulting these pastors does not help. Informing them and encouraging their superiors to place more emphasis on preaching the gospel, even when it might mean less preserving of the institution, are the things that might be of greater help to the pastors.

Other Reasons

There are other reasons why pastors appear to be less capable of handling money matters in the church than of dealing with other aspects of the church's life. One has to do with their own personal stewardship practices. A surprisingly large number of clergy feel a significant number of their fellow clergy are not good stewards of their own money. They give a relatively small amount to the church and are not good managers of their own money. Where true, this leads to a reluctance to try to help others deal with their money as good stewards.

Laity and clergy alike seem to have strong feelings that pastors often are intimidated by lay persons. One conference leader said, "It is part of a learned reaction from a few members who do not want their minister to talk about money." An Oklahoma laywoman said, "We tell our pastor, 'You look after the spiritual life of the church, and we will take care of the finances.'" To challenge this segmented and compartmentalized concept of reality may not have high priority for a pastor amidst all the many concerns and problems of a parish.

Another commonly held theory shared by both laity and clergy is that there are only so many dollars to go around. We will discuss this concept in greater depth later. However for now it should be noted that when this theory is believed by a pastor, it will affect in major ways how he or she views money in the church. A need often develops to protect the recognized "essential" ministries of the church against the financial demands that are nice but do not deal with the very existence of the institution. Every special offering and even the apportionments are seen as the enemy that threatens the payment of the vital local church program budget.

Not into Numbers

Another phenomenon in the church today seems to affect the attitude some pastors have toward money. It started as a reaction to the 1950s when great emphasis was placed on numbers, both of dollars and members. Program budgets and memberships were growing. Both were measurable and highly visible signs of success or failure. Then came the 1960s with their strong feelings of anti-institutionalism. While local church budgets continued to grow, the membership did not. Support of ministries and mission beyond the local church leveled off. Next came the 1970s with their emphasis on the "me" generation, an introspective and somewhat limited view of life.

In reaction to the overemphasis of the 1950s on numbers and in response to both the anti-institutionalism of the sixties and the introspection of the seventies, a new generation of pastors came into the church. Their basic theme was, "We're not into numbers." It was healthy to the degree that this was a corrective reaction to the fifties and a genuine emphasis on the spiritual depth and quality of the congregational life. It was hurtful to the extent that it gave these pastors a saintly excuse for a lack of involvement in matters of money and of growth.

Now ministers had a reply when asked about the failure of their congregations to pay the World Service apportionment or even to keep pace with inflation in their local church program budget. "Oh, I don't concern myself with those institutional problems. I work on the quality of our fellowship. I'm not into numbers." It sounds good, but what is really being said? How much of this claim is a true correction to an institution that became too concerned about its own life?

How much of it is an excuse for an inadequate understanding of money in the church as well as a lack of appreciation for the vital areas of Christian witness and evangelism?

To Summarize

If pastors can be helped with two attitudes, all else might become secondary, and they then might exercise good pastoral leadership in money matters. First, through lack of sound theological training pastors tend to look upon giving money as an imposition placed on the congregation rather than as an opportunity. This attitude relates to the motivation being used by the denomination to encourage giving. We will deal with that in greater detail later.

The second major factor is the pastors' serious underestimation of the ability as well as the need of their people to give to the ministries and missions of the church. In short, they do not ask enough. This misjudgment also will be subsequently discussed as we study the motivations used by the denomination to encourage giving and the real motivations that are behind every gift.

CHAPTER 8

Decisions! Decisions!

"Who makes all the decisions?" queried a woman in Tennessee as we studied the booklet describing how the denomination gathers and spends the money she and 9.6 million other members give. Who indeed! The image is of a smoothly functioning institution making decisions based on proper research and survey, channeling funds in the most efficient and effective way, and finally distributing them so as to achieve carefully considered goals and objectives.

Such an image only exists in the minds and hearts of the management experts. It in no way resembles how such a diverse, voluntary, geographically scattered entity as The United Methodist Church does its work. Yet in spite of seeming chaos and lack of efficiency or total corporate planning, the dollars end up where work needs to be done, arriving there with maximum efficiency and minimum cost. If all the work accomplished could be cataloged and evaluated, the chances are very good that it would satisfy the great majority of those who have given their money to it.

Widespread Decisions

How does it work? Unlike most giant corporations, a denomination such as The United Methodist Church has no single place where decisions are made regarding money. The decision-making process is shared among all the local churches, annual conferences, General Conference, and all their numerous agencies, boards, councils, and institutions. To further complicate matters, one must include every contributor as a part of the decision-making mechanism. How much is given and how it is spent are decisions shared by every part of this large church. No tax is levied. No demands made. In both the giving and the spending, there is a wide latitude of choice, and a multitude of options are exercised. For all the talk about distrust and suspicion, the system itself witnesses to an amazing level of trust the membership has in that system.

Out of this mix of literally millions of decisions come anticipated programs and budgets for the future. The process at every level involves decisions about finances that include some kind of negotiation between those who ask, How much is needed? and those who counter with, How much money can we expect to get? Somewhere between what is needed and what is expected to be given can be found the final answer.

This process takes place at every level of the church. The higher levels may do it with more sophistication and in a more formal manner than will a small membership rural church, but essentially these same two questions will be asked and the final decision will be made as a workable compromise between them.

Decisions at Every Level

Local churches seem now to be involving more of the membership in the formulation of their programs and supporting budgets. Persons involved in work areas and other units are asked to submit their plans. Sometimes the whole congregation is polled or given an opportunity to attend a hearing or in some other way let its views be known. All of this information then is gathered together, and the classic argument begins between the dreamers and the realists. The realists historically have been the heavy winners, stating with great gravity that, There are only so many dollars to go around! and, We have to take care of the essentials [heat and light] before we can consider those extras [missions and outreach]! They may declare, We better not turn people off by asking too much. As a final thrust, the giving level of previous years is brought forth, projections made, and a final figure is voted showing a slight increase for next year. The programs are trimmed to size with a lot of dreams not funded. The final budget then goes to the members with the hope they will consider it reasonable and will in some manner, such as pledges, indicate their willingness to support it.

This same pattern is followed at the annual conference and general levels of the denomination. The development of the programs and their needed finances may involve a more sophisticated method, including establishing goals and objectives in some complicated democratic style. Research and surveys may inform the decision makers. Yet the dynamics remain much the same as in the local church. The money needed to support the programs has to be negotiated with those who are concerned with how much money reasonably can be expected. Again, as in the local church, the more prudent and conservative usually win over the dreamers who want to accomplish "great and new" programs. The speeches made are classic and standard at all levels and highly interchangeable. We could argue that there must be better ways to make decisions, but in the final analysis, faulty as it may be, this system seems to work.

How to Raise It

Deciding program budgets is only part of the process. Also to be decided is how the funds will be raised. At the national level, it must be decided whether a program is to be funded from the World Service Fund, a special apportionment, a special day offering, or possibly the Advance. At the local level, it has to be decided whether it goes into the regular budget, whether some specific group will be asked to support it, or whether it will be cared for by a personal donation. How a program is funded finally depends on how important the decision makers consider it to be. Sometimes words and deeds seem not to match. In 1976, the General Conference solemnly declared Hunger and the Ethnic Minority Local Church to be Missional Priorities and then promptly deposited both of them in the Advance, a highly voluntary, second-mile funding channel. At the local level, more than one administrative board has declared its belief in outreach ministries, both local and worldwide, and then instructed its treasurer to wait until December to pay any benevolences and only then if there were any money left after paying the "essentials."

In spite of the best efforts of efficiency oriented persons at all levels, programs deemed important by others have a way of getting funded. The pastor of a church in North Carolina stated with pride that his church only asked people to give in one way. "We don't take special offerings or anything. It's all in the budget!" Talking with some of his members in his absence, they listed twenty-seven different funding channels open to the membership to accomplish various objectives not included in the allegedly all-inclusive program budget. These channels included the Pledge to Mission of United Methodist Women, various youth funds, a special fund for new choir robes, an adult Sunday church school class that was sponsoring a child in India, the trustees who not only handled memorial funds but were soliciting individuals to help repair the furnace, and Boy Scouts raising funds for camping. Even the pastor himself maintained a Parish Fund for emergencies and was not known to object if people put a little money into it.

One or Many

Let's consider the advantages and disadvantages of the single-line concept of giving as contrasted with the multi-channel approach. The single-line concept brings together in a single figure all the needs of the church for money, and people are then asked to give to that one item, expecting that it will care for all the programs of the church. Someone called it "putting all your begs in one ask-it!" The multichannel concept funds programs through a variety of channels in the belief that this will encourage more giving and will meet more adequately the needs of persons to select areas of personal concern.

One of the great advantages of the single-line approach is that the funds derived usually are undesignated. Decisions about their use are open to more flexibility and can be made at levels in the denomination where, according to some, more informed decisions can be made about them.

A number of persons were asked to share the degree of their agreement or disagreement with the statement When people are provided several channels for giving to the church, total monies raised tend to be higher than when channels for giving are fewer. While all respondents tended to agree with the statement, there was less agreement among national and conference leaders than among local church pastors and lay persons. A conference leader in Maine commented, "There is a cutoff point to the number of causes you can offer to people and not have confusion and the complaint that the church is always after people with another appeal."

A conference leader in Georgia said, "In my ministry I have found an increasing dislike among the laity for special offerings. They prefer a unified budget with everything in it. The best contributors pledge more when there is a unified budget." True, the *best* givers may tend to appreciate a unified approach, but the vast majority of persons in the church are not best givers. They tend to respond to multiple channels that are more likely to interest them in more focused programs. As this same Georgia officer adds, "The people whose pledges are minimal will give more when there are special offerings." Add one further note. While the inner-circle best givers tend to desire a unified approach, they, too, will respond to special offerings and other varieties of channels with money they would not otherwise have given to the single approach. Doubters should test this in their local situation sometime to see who it is that gives to special offerings.

Some of the comments of national leaders seemed to indicate a feeling that any desire by church members for multichannel or designated giving indicates a lack of trust, faith, or commitment. This may be true in some cases, but these leaders need to exercise care that they do not confuse possible lack of complete trust in the institution as some kind of lack of trust in God. There is a major difference between the two.

Same People Give to All

An interesting study was made by the Advance office over a period of several years. Each year, a survey was conducted by searching the journals of at least fifteen annual conferences to discover the relationship of giving to the Advance to that of giving to the World Service Fund. It was found that the churches that gave to the designated giving program called the Advance did a significantly better job meeting their World Service apportionment than did the churches that did not participate in the Advance. At the very least, the data seemed to indicate that there was no competition between these two funds. It might even be said that giving to the Advance encouraged giving to World Service. The study does seem to say that there are not two groups of people in the church—one seeking a single undesignated channel of giving and another seeking designated multichanneling. Rather, there is a large group of individuals and local churches who faithfully meet their World Service apportionment and then go on to seek other channels through which to support additional ministries that meet their more specific concerns.

There is a general feeling within the church that this same situation takes place within the local church. Individuals most supportive of the general program budget are the same folks who will contribute more to pay for a new organ or to repair the roof through a special offering. One man in Chico, California, talked about a drive to raise funds for a mission project. "Those who give to [that] are the givers to everything." A Decatur, Georgia, church treasurer comments, "People want options they can exercise beyond their basic support." An Atlanta pastor adds a caution. "Everybody won't give to every special offering, so don't make it a guilt trip if they don't give something."

Options Needed

At every level—local, conference, and national—there is a widespread feeling that church people need a variety of options for giving. They will accept some kind of priority rating being assigned to the various channels and methods by which they give. However once this is done, any attempt to place a duty or obligation on even the fund with the highest priority results in a negative reaction. People want to feel that what they give comes out of a sense of voluntary participation in something because of its intrinsic worth, rather than out of a sense of imposed obligation or duty.

The intense negative reaction to special offerings in some congregations may have developed because the right *not* to participate is never made clear. People feel that the only choice they have is either to give something or feel guilty.

There is a general feeling that there can be too many channels for giving. Most people know that program administrators need flexibility in funds and would be rendered inoperative if most funds came to them tightly designated or if they came from so many different channels as to be totally unpredictable. Most church members recognize that they could be overwhelmed by the sheer weight of making decisions. By the time every national, conference, and local church program came individually to every giver, there would be many thousands of options. Some kind of combining is required, or else contributors would be in an impossible situation. In making the decision to limit the number of giving channels at every level, the denomination not only uses good practical sense, but witnesses as well to its faith in the programming process.

To Summarize

Both those who work in local church administration and at higher levels of the church need to have a better understanding of the amazing level of trust the average church member manifests in the church every time a gift is given. Even with numerous funding channels available, the vast majority of program decisions are made by persons other than the individual church member. Yet this member gives support to those programs with a great amount of positive feeling. Somewhere between his trust in the program decision makers and his trust in his own personal decision making lies the truth. Room must be made for both trusts to exist.

CHAPTER 9

Duty, Obligation, Guilt, and Sacrifice

It was a great offer. He would clean my living room rug for free. I carefully explained that I had a good vacuum cleaner and was not in the market for another. He chattered away while he worked, carefully explaining the good points of his products. His work completed, his pitch went on, always polite, smiling, courteous, still talking as I all but pushed him out the door. Eyeing my sparkling clean rug, I had two overwhelming feelings—I felt guilt, and I felt obligated. His whole act was designed to put me under obligation to him and make me feel guilty if I did not buy the product.

How does the church try to get me to "buy the product"? What are the motives it appeals to? This chapter deals with how the church attempts to motivate its membership to give money. The next chapter will discuss some motivations that might get better results as well as be more in keeping with our understanding of Christian theology.

In general, the church attempts to motivate people in two ways. First, it seeks to get funds because the church needs the money. Second, the church attempts to place people under obligation and duty, makes them feel guilty if they do not give, and expects them to give sacrificially. This is a broad statement and far from true in every instance, but in general these are the motivations used when the church seeks people to transfer money from themselves to the church.

To Pay the Bills

When asked in a survey, there was almost complete agreement among pastors, lay persons, and church leaders that "giving to the church is minimal when motivated by guilt, obligation, or duty." Yet it would be interesting to examine the psychological motivations used in most of our literature and techniques for raising funds.

Another motivational technique used, on the surface, is both worthy and necessary. We ask people to give because the church needs money. "To pay the bills," responded one older layman in Alabama. He could not be shaken. That was the reason he gave, and that was OK with him. A pastor in Kansas put it more poetically. "Christ has no hands but our hands . . ." he said with a serene smile. Interview responses, survey replies, examination of local church newsletters involved in their annual fund-seeking efforts, and other data all seem to confirm it: People are asked to give money to the church because the church needs money. Further, they have an obligation and a duty to give, are guilty if they do not, and the best giving is sacrificial. There are notable exceptions to this, but across the denomination this seems to be the pattern of motivation used to elicit money from the membership.

The church *does* need money to survive. No one would argue with that fact. But all too often, there is a subtle inference that goes beyond the survival of the institution. It is implied that not only does the church need the money to survive, but so does the kingdom of God—". . . no hands but our hands," we recite with a great deal more poetic license than good theology. The ancient Greeks believed that a god ceased to exist upon the death or defection of his/her last worshiper. Do we as Christians really believe that Christ and his kingdom depend on what we put in the offering plate? The evidence seems to be that while we may not come right out and say we believe it, we do imply it and subtly teach it in the way we try to motivate people to give.

Self-Fulfillment

If the primary motivation used to encourage people to give is because the church needs money, it would seem to create some very interesting psychological dynamics. The giver gives, and the church receives. The church gets, and the giver gives up. The giver is losing something—giving it up, making a sacrifice.

One wonders if at its best the Christian faith is a self-denying faith or a self-fulfilling faith. Jesus did talk about denying oneself. Sacrifice is biblical through and through. However, the implication is that Jesus was talking about denying oneself of a lesser thing in order to achieve a higher thing *for oneself*. One wonders how many Christians see it that way when asked to make their giving sacrificial. "Why, sacrificial giving is giving that hurts!" explained one Virginian when asked what was meant by sacrifice. Do we really sacrifice by following Christ, by attending worship, by attempting to be faithful to the Christian ethic, or by giving money?

A veteran missionary talked about his sacrifice with regret. "I served over thirty years with a feeling that to serve Christ meant to give up everything I really wanted. Then came a group of young joyous missionaries whose whole motivation was in the other direction. They told me they didn't feel they were giving up a thing by serving Christ as missionaries. They weren't giving up their lives. They were finding life!" With a wistful sadness he added, "I wish I had served on those terms."

Unlike some world religions, Christianity at its best has not been a faith that denied life but fulfilled it. One wonders whether talk about self-denial or sacrifice in relation to giving

money really is understood in Christian terms or whether it
might imply a negative self-denial that takes from giving the
joy it deserves.

Duty and Obligation

Why should one give to the church? Because one has a duty
and an obligation to give seems to be the general reply across
the church. "Will you be loyal to The United Methodist
Church and uphold it by your prayers, your presence, your
gifts, and your service?" Many times it was pointed out by the
laity and clergy alike that, after all, the members did promise
to give when they joined.

The logic is now complete. The church needs money, and
the membership has promised to give it. As a layman from
Florida wrote, "I feel there is a certain obligation or duty that
every Christian undertakes as a member of [the] church." A
conference leader from Ohio adds, "What's wrong with
obligation or duty? We have 'graced' ourselves out of business
in too many instances. I do a lot of things out of obligation or
duty, nor do I resent it." A pastor in Minnesota puts it, "A
little guilt and duty helps."

One could argue that possibly the real argument is not
about duty and obligation, but whether that duty and
obligation are externally imposed or whether they arise out of
an inner obedience to a sensed need for self-fulfillment which
in turn requires the discipline of duty. A sensitive awareness
of how obligation can be a positive force in life was explained
by a group of Japanese Americans. One woman explained,
"For the Japanese, obligation and duty are an important part
of the culture, so for many people in our church they may be
motivations." The group explained that discharging an
obligation was a major way in which they found great
personal fulfillment. They did not see it as something
externally imposed but as coming out of their own keen

desire to feel fulfilled as Christians and as Japanese. There was a positive feeling about the way they sensed obligation, which was not present in the heavy, externally imposed obligation explained in other settings.

While, in general, those in the church believe that making people feel obligated may not be the highest Christian motivation, they concede that it does get results. A pastor in Texas commented, "Many arch-conservatives raise large sums appealing to guilt, duty, or fear—*NOT* that we should join them." A conference leader in Indiana: ". . . the guilt boys get the dollars." A pastor in Arkansas wrote, "The conservative churches are doing far better [than we], and the prod of guilt, obligation, and duty is their chief weapon."

There is some recognition in the church that while these motivations may get results for a while, they probably will be both minimal and short-term. A national leader shared that she thinks, "duty and obligation are factors in giving. Guilt often backfires and is not long lasting. There are too many guilt trips in all areas of the church." A conference leader confessed, "I would sure hate to lose the money given to the church because of guilt, obligation, or duty, but there are higher motives." It probably is one of the ironies of all time that the church—the one community which has been called into existence to proclaim the dissolution of guilt as humanity's most anxious burden—is in the business of seeking money by deliberately provoking people to feel guilty.

We could debate a long time whether it is proper to motivate Christians to give money to the church out of a sense of duty or obligation or guilt. However, the more pragmatic question remains as to whether it works. Does it really raise money? In certain parts of the church, it not only works but works well. Churches that are rural, small, and have a minimum turnover in membership seem to continue to be successful in raising funds by stressing these motivating factors. A woman in western North Carolina shared how her family had been part of the same small rural church for over six generations. She let it be known that her loyalty to the church as an institution transcended any concern for what the church might or might not be accomplishing through its program. Her reason for giving was straightforward. "I feel obligated. I have a duty." This strong sense of duty to the institution also could be sensed in a number of ethnic congregations. There is no doubt that in some situations money does come in response to (1) the need of the church for it and (2) a sense of obligation and duty on the part of the members to give it.

Through, Not To

There is, however, an increasing portion of the church in which a plea to support the institution out of a sense of duty will tend to minimize the response. Members in local churches that are urban, larger, and have a younger and more transient membership will not be highly motivated by a plea for institutional support or by reminding them of their duty or obligation as members to give their money. There will be a much greater interest in what ministries the church is accomplishing. A classic statement was made by a layman in Mississippi who was a member of a large urban church. "I don't give *to* the church as much as I give *through* the church." That statement is well worth considering. It seems to say something important about how we motivate our membership as we move into our third century.

In discussing what motivates people to give money to voluntary charities, most professional fund raisers are in agreement that the "ought" is out. It is becoming much more difficult to raise funds out of some sense of moral obligation, institutional loyalty, or fear of feeling guilty if one does not give. The consensus is that funds can be raised in this manner, but they tend to be minimal. One fundraiser for a national charity explained, "They will give but only enough to get you off their backs. Their motive in giving will not be to feel involved in what your agency is doing but to get rid of you. Their gift is not 'buying in,' but buying their way out."

If the vacuum cleaner salesman had some product for a dollar, I would have bought it. Anything to get him off my back. Or to be more honest, anything to get rid of my feelings of obligation and the consequent guilt. Many professional fundraisers believe that people indeed will give out of a sense of guilt, but it will be just enough to cancel the feeling and no more. There is a good chance they will do a lot of dodging before they ever get themselves into a feeling of obligation again. One may bail out a boat because of a sense of duty and obligation, but somehow it lacks the joy and fulfillment of setting the sails and moving across the waters. Possibly out of our survival syndrome we have settled for the bailing and have forgotten that the vast majority of our people are not only capable of setting sails but have a keen need and desire to be about it. As one pastor put it, "Duty speaks of the push of the past instead of the pull of the future."

Duty, obligation, sacrifice—words that have moved mountains and converted nations. This is no attempt to consign them to the totally negative side of life or theology, but only to say that as we move into our third century the time may have come to seek other more fulfilling ways to stimulate participation in what can be done through the church. We are deeply indebted to those who came before and often with little joy bailed the boat in the hope that someday other more fortunate people could set the sails. A Mississippi pastor talked about the passing of such a generation whose loyalty and sense of duty enabled the church, not only to survive, but often to grow and to flourish. "So many people of that generation are dying, but their depth of loyalty was so great that even as they die they make sure the church gets its money. [They had] the kind of love where they would just about do anything for the church to make sure that the needs were going to be met." He added sadly that he does not see that kind of commitment continuing. "It was of another era."

Peer Pressure

One other motivation—peer pressure—needs to be mentioned here. How am I doing compared to others? No district superintendent wants to have the lowest figures in the cabinet when payment of apportionments is totaled. The same comparisons are made among pastors and bishops. Church members generally are not obvious in their comparative giving, but with the clergy the expectations of others play a part. A very few churches even list pledges and consequent payments on bulletin boards—a practice which does not meet universal approval. Is peer pressure a worthy motivation? If the gospel speaks of a sense of self-worth that derives from God's love, then peer pressure is a doubtful motivation for Christians. Does it get results? Yes, it helps pull up the lowest givers.

In most fund drives the experts counsel to have the big givers give first, and then let others know that this huge amount has been given by these few people. Many times the campaign committee and the pastor will give first, and it will be announced that so many pledges resulted in so many dollars pledged, usually an amount much larger than the average gift will be. There is a genuine need, especially for those new to the faith, to have some guidance as to what level of giving is expected. However, peer pressure can quickly translate into a sense of obligation imposed from outside and tends to wear thin in time.

To Summarize

As we face a new future, we need to ask serious questions about the traditional ways in which we have tried to motivate people to give money to the church. Is pleading for institutional support the best way in a day when there is increasing anti-institutionalism as well as resistance to the institutionalizing process? In a day when people are increasingly transient, urban, and desirous of being involved in decision-making, is seeking a response out of duty or obligation the way to get the best results? In a time when people increasingly seek to find avenues through which they can be fulfilled as persons, is talk of sacrifice and self-denial the best way to encourage people to give? As we move into our third century, there may be other motivations that are not only going to result in more money being given but might be more Christian as well.

CHAPTER 10

What's in It for Me?

Why do people give money to the church? The church attempts in many instances to motivate people to give in ways that may or may not match how people actually are motivated. If the combination of motivating through (1) the need for the institution to receive money rather than the need for the individual to give it, (2) a sense of duty and obligation, (3) implied guilt for little or no giving, and (4) a stress on sacrifice does constitute the ways in which the church is motivating people to give, we may be working in direct opposition to the manner in which people seek to be motivated.

Pay the Bills

Remember the man who when asked why he gave money to the church replied, "To pay the bills." Nothing would budge him. As far as he was concerned, all the talk about gratitude or anything else was "preacher talk." Money was given so that the bills could be paid and that was that. "But suppose your pastor found a way to get all those bills paid," I challenged. I went on to build a hypothetical situation in which some anonymous person agreed to pay all the bills and would not ask anything in return except that no one else would be allowed to give any money to the church. "Would that be OK with you?" I inquired. His eyebrows went straight up. "Never!" he roared. Just the idea of it made it difficult for him to talk. Finally, he sat back and looked down at his hands. "You just took my church away from me," he mumbled.

"I'd be tempted!" was the laughing reply of a hardworking local church treasurer when the same hypothetical situation was shared with her. Then she quickly added, "No, if that were done I'd have to move my membership. I need to give to live." Lay people in New England shared horror stories about neighboring churches that were given large endowments and no longer required their people to give. "That is worse than not having any money," was the response of one upstate New Yorker.

Even in the Asian congregation where obligation is a strong and noble concept, there was a feeling that giving money was more than institutional support or the discharge of duty. A woman in San Jose explained that her giving was on two levels—a pledge and the giving of offerings. "The pledge is for the church itself," she explained. "The offering is something between God and me. It is the offering where the caring and the sharing come across."

Meeting with groups and individuals across the church, nothing aroused such strong reaction as when this hypothetical possibility was suggested. Even the "bill payers" strongly implied that giving money to the church was an act that had deep personal meaning far beyond merely meeting an obligation or maintaining the institution. It is no accident or empty tradition that the offering continues as the high moment of symbolic dedication in most worship experiences.

Gratitude

Gratitude was mentioned again and again as a primary motivation for giving. We love because he first loved us. An awareness of the gift of life through Christ was articulated especially by clergy and by laity who are church leaders, usually with a guilt free, positive identification of gratitude.

As one Ohio laywoman commented, "To be a good giver one must first be a good getter."

However, all too often there was a feeling on the part of church leaders that others *ought* to be grateful and that lack of giving was proof of lack of gratitude. When gratitude is imposed as a duty, a serious question is raised as to whether it remains as gratitude and whether it serves as a positive motivation for giving money or anything else. Like other motives, gratitude remains positive only as it comes out of the internal life, rather than being imposed as requirement or duty.

Self-Concern

Many persons involved in raising money for national charities, universities, and for the church believe that behind every voluntary gift is a basic question people will ask. That question is, What's in it for me? At almost every level of the church, when this concept was shared the reaction was strongly negative. Various groups were asked, "What would you think if you called on a new family in your congregation to obtain a pledge and they asked you, 'What's in it for me?'" One indignant South Carolinian retorted, "Why would such a person even belong to a Christian church?" A national leader stated that such a question implies a person is "hedonistic and selfish, certainly not Christian!"

An Ohio pastor replied, "I would be surprised at an active member asking such a question." A Dallas layman: "That [statement] hurts me. I am repulsed by it." The wording of the question, What's in it for me? seemed to conjure up images of selfish people seeking to gain materially and concerned only with their own self-satisfactions. Not everyone reacted negatively. A seminary professor responded in a different way. "I see it akin to the question asked Jesus, 'What must I do to inherit eternal life?' which is not necessarily a selfish or even self-centered question but came out of a healthy self-concern."

A woman in New Mexico said, "Most people give out of a sincere desire to find a way to fulfill their own lives." Self-fulfillment in the Christian sense is *not* instant gratification. It is *not* self-indulgence at the expense of others. It is *not* introspective selfishness. Rather, it is the attempt to participate in what is understood to be ultimately real and supremely significant, in what Christians refer to as the kingdom of God. It is a synthesis of self-denial and self-actualization—the discovery of what it means to be first by being last, and being the greatest by being the servant. It is the quest for salvation in its most intensive private sense and in its most positive social sense.

What People Seek

Why this search for self-fulfillment? There seems to be general agreement across the church that our present age is becoming increasingly unfulfilling. "I feel constantly dehumanized" was how a college student in Oklahoma put it. "The arena in which I can make decisions about my own life and world is constantly growing smaller," wrote a district superintendent in Missouri. The encroachment of systems, government, the media, and life in general seems to be creating a feeling on the part of most people that they no longer are in charge of meaningful parts of their own lives. They feel it is beyond their ability to influence world events in any significant way.

Christians constantly are being told that they are persons of value and of infinite worth. This may be good news, but where is the arena in which they can act out this infinite worth? Even in areas of benevolence and charity, they find a systemic presence that smacks of less and less personal involvement.

It is precisely at this point that the church today is presented with its greatest opportunity. It well may represent one of the few places in which people in community can find personal involvement that provides channels of real and significant personal fulfillment.

Go back again to that person who gave to the church just "to pay the bills." When a hypothetical way was found to pay those bills without him, he experienced real grief. "You have taken my church away from me." What was meant by that? He was expressing a felt need in people all over the church.

The need for the church to receive is exceeded by the need for the vast majority of its members to give. "I could never be happy just being preoccupied with myself and my wants," reflected a layman in California. "I've got to be working for something bigger." A laywoman in Maryland confided, "I'll tell you the truth. I feel the church connects me with my world. I get real personal satisfaction in having an impact, however small, in matters crucial to my world."

These are not statements of self-centered, selfish people. They are the reflections of persons who are informed and inspired by the gospel and who are looking for ways to be fulfilled and complete. "It may sound pretentious, but I feel some kind of connection with the Christians of earlier days who tried to make this a better world" was the comment of a black pastor in a small, rural, southern church way out in the piney woods, as he talked about the money he gives to his church. "And it links me to this whole world and to future Christians who will be working on the same things. I'm grateful to be a part of that."

What is it people seek when they give money to church or charity? In a world that is growing increasingly directive in how money is used, giving to church or charity becomes the most voluntary financial decision many people make. It could be argued that payment of everything from taxes to mortgages constitutes a voluntary act. Yet the degree of social, legal, and other pressures are much heavier on almost every other financial decision than they are on the part of their money that people give to church and charity.

Voluntary Decisions

This "voluntary" aspect to giving may constitute one of our strongest motivations to give. In this highly developed, increasingly circumscribed society, the arena in which decisions can be made by individuals about their own lives is definitely narrowing. Gone are the days when we could leisurely drive a buggy down the country lane. Modern highways require obedience to speed laws, lights, signs, lanes, and other restrictions.

Most decisions that constrain our freedom and decide our future seem to be made in places and by persons remote from our influence and control. We have a feeling of being held hostage by superpowers in their deadly game of nuclear chess. More and more of our compensation for work is not in our control but comes in the form of such predetermined things as pensions, hospital insurance, and withheld taxes. Personal funds over which people can exercise personal discretion are further reduced as they face mortgage payments, grocery bills, tuition payments, and energy costs. Psychologically, people feel hemmed in. They feel that they have lost control of their own lives. A feeling of worthlessness results. To counter this feeling, they seek avenues through which they can derive some sense of personal worth, involvement, and fulfillment.

It is at this very point that the church with its multitude of worthwhile programs can provide ways through which self-fulfillment can take place. A farmer in Kansas commented about the money he gives the church. "It's an opportunity to participate on a grand scale with other people." In listening to him, one felt that there was no sense of sacrifice on his part. Instead, he was buying into something that gave him a deep sense of personal fulfillment.

Earlier, there was mention of a question that many professional fund raisers believe is back of every charitable gift. What's in it for me? On the surface such a question seems the very antithesis of Christian commitment. If so, one must ask whether the Christian faith calls on its followers to deny their own sense of self-worth or whether it calls for them to seek self-fulfillment in ways that are informed by the gospel. If the latter is true, then it may be that this question takes on a different form for the Christian. How can giving my money to the church help me fulfill my life as a follower of Christ? How can it give me a feeling and a reality of my own worth as a child of God?

In discussions with individuals and groups across the church, this need for self-fulfillment presented itself again and again. It came from every region and from people of all racial and ethnic groups, all ages, and every economic level. In essence, each was asking, "How can I make decisions that make a difference in my own life and in the world?" What agency can match the church for presenting people with a way to satisfy that deep need? The basic thrust of our motivations should move from support of an institution to an emphasis in which people believe they are participating in a fulfilling ministry. This ministry should be seen as global in nature, profoundly centered in things that really matter, and concerned not only with doing things for others but also in providing ways in which one's own personal worth and dignity can be achieved.

Not Understood by Leaders

While there is a general desire within the church to contribute because of this sense of sharing in a fulfilling ministry, there seems to be a lack of understanding on the part of some church leaders that such a motivation is there. A group of major decision makers in a church agency was asked, "What do you expect to happen in the lives of people who give money to this agency?" The silence that followed was long, profound, and embarrassing. These leaders gave much thought to what would be done with the money given, and they considered what might happen to persons who would receive the services the money would make possible. Yet little if any thought had been given to what happens in the lives of those who give the money. Such a group of leaders is not to be criticized. However, it just might be that the effectiveness of their programs would be enhanced, and the funds received might be increased if there were concern for the giver along with a rightful concern for the recipients.

In a society that continually narrows the arena in which the individual can make decisions about his or her personal life, community, and world, the ability to make decisions somewhere becomes increasingly important. It is not enough just to become involved in serving or giving to programs conceived by someone else. People need to have some point at which they, too, can be involved in making decisions about what might happen. Many local churches are discovering the value of involving the membership in developing the program before they invite them to underwrite it financially. This involvement may or may not result in the program containing everything an individual wants done. Often, being involved in deciding is enough. At least the persons' views were considered. They have participation in the program. Now, when financial participation is offered it is not just participation in someone else's program but their own program as well.

The tendency of the decision makers at every level in the church is to resist this desire by the general membership for some voice in deciding what is done. "Trust and obey, for there's no other way" may be applicable to our relationship to our Lord, but other ways are available by which the general membership and the decision makers can relate to each other. The latter have decisions to make, and the energy expended involving others in the process smacks of inefficiency as well as a challenge to their power. Yet in the long pull, shared participation not only serves the best interest of those with whom it is shared but results in their greater willingness to put their money and interest into the resulting program. To restate, people are not looking just for a place to make decisions but for places where their decisions can involve them in creative and fulfilling activities.

Participation in programs is not easily shared. One national staff person, in explaining why she was involved in interpreting an agency to the church, put it this way: "We need to let them know what *we* are doing and how the church supports *our* work." Possibly a more sensitive explanation would be, We need to let them know what *they* are doing in Christian ministry *through* this agency. Changing the words is not as important as changing the attitude behind the words.

Still Much Trust

Obviously, not everyone can be involved in every decision the denomination makes concerning how money is spent. No one is asking for this. Possibly what they are seeking has a touch of Rodney Dangerfield in it—a plea that somewhere someone will give them some respect. Also, the people of the church are highly motivated by a desire to show their loyalty to and trust in the church. Sometimes this loyalty takes some strange twists. One Tennessee layman said that the major reason why his church paid its apportionments was "to keep our preacher out of trouble with the conference." This motivation for paying things beyond the local church was heard more often in my research than I would have preferred. Even if this was less than the desired motivation, it expressed a sense of loyalty and even love that should not be totally put down.

The stress on the need for persons to find personal fulfillment through giving does not eliminate a need to be aware of what they are giving to. Some years ago, there was a movement in the church for local congregations to seek pledges first and then to build their program budgets next. The theory was that people need to witness to a basic trust in the church. The movement is not as strong today as it was a few years back. Most churches have gone back to program building first and then asking for pledges.

Why did this other system seem not to work? Possibly, it did not give sufficient attention to the current general disinterest in institutional loyalty. It called on a primary loyalty to the local church as an institution rather than a desire to participate through the local church in its programs. Longtime loyal members certainly would have no difficulty responding to this approach. Their experience would have taught them that they could count on the church to develop an acceptable program, even if it was after pledging had taken place.

Younger and newer members might be more hesitant. After all, the church itself has preached about the sacredness of all God's world. It just might be that there are also other agencies through which God's will could be done and through which people could feel a sense of personal fulfillment. In short, much more now than a hundred years ago, the church is in competition with many other institutions and agencies in presenting programs that Christians find personally fulfilling and in which they want to place their dollars. By returning first to building the basic program and then seeking pledged participation, people are presented with data they need in order to understand fully what they are participating in. It helps them feel they have made the wisest choice in choosing this channel for their giving.

Involvement Needed

Being involved in some kind of process in which people are allowed to have an influence on the shape of the church's program is fulfilling and thus serves as an excellent motivation to giving. There also are strong feelings in the church for providing other options in addition to the basic program budget.

The United Methodist Church has been very wise in providing such options at every level of its life. Special offerings, the Advance, Supplementary Gifts, and other channels allow individuals and local churches to exercise their special interests and concerns. It allows for special interest groups and persons with special interests to invest themselves more fully in those interests than the total body would care to do. Only those who believe there are limited dollars in the church feel that these options are a threat to the basic program funds. The evidence seems to indicate that the opposite is true—those who find channels for exercising their special interests are the persons who are the most supportive of the basic program budget.

If people do not find these options available to them in the church, they will look for them elsewhere. Why do they want them? "I think God speaks to me here in Detroit as much as he speaks to those folks in New York or Nashville" was one laywoman's response. She is also a firm advocate of her church's program budget, of World Service, and of Women's Pledge to Missions. Her desire for options through which she was able to exercise her special concerns was not in competition with her trust in the system and strong support of general giving. As an Oklahoma farmer said, "I not only have a right to make some decisions for myself, but I believe God has demanded I do so."

The sad note is that all too often the availability of authorized options is not shared with the membership. This is because pastors and other decision makers in the local churches fear that since, in their opinion, only a limited number of dollars is available, people would select among the options at the expense of their basic pledge. Possibly no single concept limits the number of dollars available to the church more than the belief that only limited dollars are available.

Do Not Have to Give

Another strong motivation for giving is the belief that you do not have to give. This could be called grace-full stewardship. It is best illustrated by a variety of negative opinions people shared about special offerings. "We don't have them. We stick them in the budget." "People don't like always being asked for money." Possibly the comment that best explains the negative attitude toward such offerings was "I hate to be made to feel guilty!" It may be that most negative feelings about special offerings result from a duty/obligation/guilt approach that causes people to give to special offerings in self-defense to avoid a sense of guilt. No one likes to feel guilty every other Sunday, so the best defense is a good offense—ban the offerings.

One church, interdenominational in character and organization, received twenty-six special offerings a year—one every two weeks. This happened because they were related to several denominations, all of which had special offerings. Little complaining was heard in the congregation. Over the years, members had been helped to understand that no one was expected to give to every offering or even to any of them. They were urged to give only to those things in which they had an interest and through which they believed they would feel a sense of fulfillment. This approach worked.

Permission not to give—sincerely urging people not to participate unless they can do it with a sense of gladness and fulfillment—seems antithetical to successful fund-raising.

Yet it allows people to feel free to make their own decisions about their financial participation, whether for special offerings or the basic budget. As a seminary professor said, "We believe in grace except in finances. Then we believe in basic Old Testament law and good old-fashioned guilt!"

Trust of the System

Along with a need to be involved in decision-making and a need for options to participate in freely chosen special interests, people are motivated to give when they trust the delivery systems. In the Advance program, an acknowledgment of every gift is required by *The Book of Discipline*. Some who harbor suspicions about any designated giving program claim that the donors demand an acknowledgment because they want to be thanked. Those more closely related to the program and supportive of it feel that the acknowledgment is important for very different reasons.

Donors do not want to be thanked. They want three other things acknowledged. First, did the gift get there? Second, did it do any good? Third, is more needed? These are valid questions in today's world unless one equates faith in God with blind acceptance of the efficiency and impeccability of every religious organization.

Some churches and charities in recent years have been known to deliver less than a reasonable proportion of the gift to the place of service. Even the most honest organization will, at times, misdirect funds. Both honest error and less-than-honest systems have made people wary of uncritical acceptance, even of their own church. The United Methodist Church should welcome such testing of its systems of fund delivery.

Through years of exprience, honest administration, well-developed accounting systems, and possibly a bit of good luck, the denomination is able to move billions of dollars from millions of donors to thousands of particular programs and projects with timely efficiency and minimum cost. The system passes the test under the closest scrutiny. In today's world, the ability to commend the delivery system as well as the program to be funded is vital in motivating people to give.

To Summarize

Christians want to give. They know they need to give, not because they are commanded to do so, but because the very wellspring of their being cries out to be significantly involved in things that matter. The ability to do this must be an act of free will. To be involved in a way that fulfills the quest of the spirit for participation in the eternal things in life—that is what motivates the people of God. "What must I do to inherit eternal life?" What's in it for me?

CHAPTER 11

To Pledge or Not to Pledge

"If we tried to get pledges, we'd lose half our income!" She was the pastor of a three-point charge in the Appalachian Mountains. Her comment may come as a surprise to those who serve or belong to large urban churches and who assume that everyone everywhere pledges to the church or makes some kind of annual estimate. Not so. Most United Methodists pledge, but most United Methodist churches do not ask them to. Of all United Methodist local churches, 64 percent have less than two hundred members. But these same churches contain only 22 percent of the total United Methodist membership. The majority of these smaller, mostly rural churches still resist the pledge as a way to raise funds. As one North Carolina layman explained, "They don't want to make a promise they can't keep."

We need to remember that it is the local church from which all the money comes. Even that small percentage of persons who fund agencies in some direct way, whether current or deferred, usually are local church members and inclined to be motivated and informed by what happens locally. What systems do United Methodist churches use to undergird their programs financially?

Many Ways

You name it, someone is doing it! A five-thousand-member church in Texas gathers pledges first and then makes up its program budget. A rural church in upper New York never mentions money until it is at least $5,000 behind; then it advertises its needs from pulpit and newsletter. Leaders of a church in Oregon visit homes *before* the program is planned to get everyone's ideas; then call again to gather the pledges. A church in North Carolina has five men who have made all the financial decisions for as long as anyone can remember. A North Carolina layman explained, "Treasurers usually start talking to people when bills accumulate."

More Help Plan

However, there is a decided trend toward involving more people in planning the church program. That not only gives a larger number of persons a sense of participation in the eventual success of funding the program, but much to the inner circle's surprise, good ideas result from this broader-based planning. There is real value in providing some process through which more members can claim the church's program as their own.

Once the program is planned, whether formally or informally by the leadership group, the next step is to obtain some kind of pledge, estimate of giving, or other clue as to how much money can be expected. Every Member Visitation, Circuit Rider, Pony Express, professional fund-raiser, Dedication Sunday, pledge dinner, special letter, sermon, and all the rest are used. Yet no technique is as important as the attitude with which it is done.

Begging and Neglect

All over the church, people commented about two common feelings they have experienced in local church fund-raising attempts. "When we try to recruit people to call in homes for pledges, they tell us they don't like to beg for money," said one local finance chairperson in Ohio. "When I call, what I hear more than anything else is that all we want from them is their money," commented an old hand at finance campaigns in Missouri. Why are these two feelings so universal? People do not like to beg, and those called on feel that all that is really wanted is their money. Both feelings may reflect a reality. People *are* sent out to beg and money *is* what is really wanted.

"I always felt I was taking something from them," was the reaction of a layman in California. "No one ever told me I was offering them a great product." St. Francis may have been exhilarated by being the Lord's beggar, but it does not sit too well with most United Methodists. Calling at best is not easy. A seminarian defended the attitudes of finance callers, "They meet people who are rude and unpleasant. Many aren't home. Some have the attitude that they shouldn't give. Others are invalids, old, or just plain poor!" True, but even these experiences are bearable so long as the caller believes something is being offered to people instead of taken from them.

Could it be that all we *really* want from them is their money? If the major emphasis is on the need of the church to receive rather than the need for the individual to participate, then the subtle unintended message is that, Yes, the money is what is important. This message often is reinforced by the call for money being the only call some persons receive from the church.

If Only

All across the church there is a wistful yearning for a kind of fund-gathering that could be called the *If Only* technique. "*If only* everybody would tithe," grumbled a retired New Mexico pastor. "*If only* they would just give and not have to be asked," sighed a battle weary finance chairperson from Illinois.

Tithing seems to be the favorite *If only* method recommended. Many pastors and lay persons shared their joy in the practice. "It is the *only* way to give," exclaimed a young Kansas minister. Usually, as the tithers extolled tithing's values others in the same group would be very quiet. They were the non-tithers, obviously representing the overwhelming majority of the church. They were fearful that they were about to be made to feel guilty because they did not tithe. Often that is precisely what does happen.

For all its virtues, the tithe seems to be explained more often as a duty, a law to be obeyed, rather than as a means of experiencing grace. As a California layman replied when asked if people in his church accept the tithe as a guide to giving, "Nobody's brought it up to be rejected." This way of giving is stressed in the Rio Grande Conference, in Puerto Rico, in smaller more rural churches, but the evidence seems to be that only a small minority of the membership tithes, that the tithe is not being strongly advocated today, and that the practice probably is decreasing. This decrease is good if the tithe represents law more than grace. Where it can be recommended as a guide to a more joyous voluntary participation, may it increase.

Positive Giving

So the money is given—some pledged and some not, some because it was begged and some with a feeling of personal fulfillment, some in a full measure and overflowing and some so small a gift that it merely serves as an immunization against further attacks. Most of it is given with positive attitudes. "That's one thing I can do," commented a layman in Mississippi. "I may fail in other areas, but I can usually give what I said I would."

It needs to be said here that there is no such thing as a typical giver or an average gift in a denomination as diverse as this. A pastor in Texas shared a formula. He said that 5 percent of the members give 25 percent of the funds. Another 10 percent give another 25 percent. The third 25 percent comes from an additional 20 percent of the members. Finally, the remaining 65 percent give only the 25 percent balance of the funds. If this formula is true throughout the denomination, then in 1979 about half-a-million members gave an average of about $775 each for the year. At the other end of the scale, over 9.2 million members gave only about $60 each for the year. Play the *If only* game and consider what the church's total income would be *if only* everyone gave as did the top 5 percent. The church would have received a total of over $7.4 billion in 1979 instead of only $1.5 billion.

The reality is that all people do not give alike. Growth is required as they move from a gift that comes from a sense of duty and obligation to one that comes from joyful participation. This growth comes only as the church shares with them a motivation based on their need to give instead of just telling them about the church's need to receive.

Seek Guidance

As members grow in their benevolent attitude, they will seek guidance as to how to give. Other worthy causes will offer them avenues to service: United Good Neighbors, Red Cross, etc. The church well may serve them best by demonstrating what it is doing instead of insisting on a top priority among worthy causes. It is valid to say to the bottom 65 percent of givers that those who give more are finding it to be a fulfilling, gratifying experience. People do seek guidance about what amount is appropriate so long as it is shared without some kind of judgment attached.

To Summarize

Pledge, no pledge, Pony Express, Circuit Rider, Every Member Visitation, the gum-tree meeting—the myriad ways in which the denomination's funds are sought are wonderful to behold. Of more consequence are the attitudes and motivations with which they are raised. An Oklahoma pastor confessed, "I used to tell them in so many words that poor old God was in trouble and needed their help. Now I tell them the church has the best bargain in town. It offers them participation in the kingdom of God, the mighty works of the Lord, here and everywhere. You can't beat a deal like that!"

CHAPTER 12

I Love to Tell the Story!

A promotion staff person from a general agency put it this way, "I believe that for every task the church needs to do there are people in the church willing and able to provide the energy to get it done." He added that he saw his job as getting the program and the people in touch with each other. "That isn't always so easy."

Materials

"Why does the church send me all this garbage?" complained a Wisconsin pastor waving a handful of leaflets. "Most of it goes in the wastebasket!" A little later he again was on his feet. "How can you expect us to support programs if you don't give us information about them?" Contradictory? Maybe so, but this reflects a reality with more than just a few pastors and members. The ability of The United Methodist Church to produce leaflets, brochures, filmstrips, and other communication devices is second to none in all Christendom. The ability to get them used is another story. "I see stacks and stacks of unused stuff," moaned a national promotion officer, "in conference offices, pastor's studies, and down in all kinds of basements."

The denomination spends several millions of dollars each year on efforts to educate, communicate, and promote—trying to get programs and people in touch with each other. United Methodist Communications budgeted $2,563,000 in

1981 to promote all the national funds. Every general agency, every church institution, and every annual conference has money budgeted for this job. Local churches grind out newsletters and bulletins, put up posterboards and signs, and send out special letters to get the word around.

It needs to be said here that expenditure for education and promotion is far from being a waste. It goes beyond getting funds for programs. To educate, sensitize, and hopefully involve the membership is a major part of what it means to be the church. The need to communicate transcends the need for persons to participate financially and for programs to receive funds. How well do we accomplish the task?

"If they are educated they will give!" It is that simple according to a conference United Methodist Women president. A Colorado rancher had a different opinion. "If they know what's happening, one of two things will result—they'll either support it or they won't." Possibly education is not the panacea some believe it to be for gaining finances, but it is a priority need if the church is truly to be the church.

Do our communication and education efforts get the job done? A layman from Herman, Nebraska, comments, "I do think the United Methodist explanations concerning missions, apportionments, etc. have been too wordy and complicated for most lay and clergy people to take the time to go through. Our financial needs and expressions need to be simpler, less wordy, and common to everyday experience."

Less Institution

Another comment heard frequently is about the heavy emphasis on the institution. "Look at this," complained a woman in Georgia about a piece of literature. "It says, 'The United Methodist church is doing such and such.' Why don't they say, '*You* are doing such and such *through* the church?'"

This is a point worth considering. The interest is in what is being done, not who is doing it. The members want to know what they are doing *through* the church, not what some agency is doing. Most people do not respond favorably to the felt need of church agencies to explain their existence. They do express appreciation for literature that emphasizes programs and the way in which the readers can relate to them.

If the promotion staff person is correct in saying that there is a supportive audience somewhere in the church for every task the church needs to do, it might be a good idea for the church to spend less time with a scattershot approach in its promotion and more time finding and informing specific audiences. The computer provides the technology for finding and informing specific audiences about specific programs.

Share Support

Support is always a consideration in promotion. Who supports what programs? The implied premise in most promotional materials is that denomination-wide programs are the property of general agencies, conference programs are the promotional responsibility of conference personnel, and the local church manages only its own programs. The so-called supporting audience is, however, *all* in the local church. Ultimately, the final goal is to speak to those 9.7 million United Methodist members about *their* programs— whether local, conference, national, or worldwide.

A good example of the failure to speak to that final audience at its level is found in the familiar pie chart about the World Service Fund turned out faithfully each quadrennium by the denomination's promotion office. By the time it gets to the local church, it is useless. At that level, the World Service apportionment has been combined with conference benevolences into a single apportionment to the local church. Would it not be more effective for the denomination's promotion agency to help annual conferences turn out a pie chart or some other means of communication that combines both World Service and conference benevolences?

Are there ways in which all this vast promotional energy can be used to help local churches see national and conference programs as an extension of their own local church ministries, so that the membership identifies them as "our programs"? What is promoted as property of others usually will come out as *obligation*. What is promoted as something *we* are doing will be accepted much more as *opportunity*. Possibly more energy needs to be spent by promotional agencies at every level to help those in the levels immediately below them do a more effective task.

Will It Fly?

It generally is believed that the majority of the members do not have a good understanding of how the denomination works beyond the local church. It is a matter of some debate whether most members really need to know. Their more basic need is to trust that the organization will operate properly and will help them do what they want to do. Will it do the job?

Do the vast programs of the larger church fulfill my need to be involved in what Christ is doing out there? This knowledge and assurance will be communicated when local churches begin to claim these programs as extensions of their own ministry and mission instead of viewing them as an obligation and an obligatory responsibility placed on them to support what others are doing.

Communication

As the church grows more sophisticated at all levels, both in its perception of Christian ministry and mission and in its ability to communicate, there is a greater need to transmit information between the various units of the church at every level. What are others doing? Each annual conference needs to hear what seventy-two other annual conferences are doing both in terms of programs and how they are promoted. The same is true between local churches. The day in which big pitchers (general agencies) poured knowledge and know-how into smaller pitchers (annual conferences and local churches) is fast disappearing. The qualitative and quantitative source for new ideas in the areas of both program and promotion will increasingly be as much at these lower levels as at the national level. Communicating information about the dynamic ministries that are happening all over the church at every level currently is very limited. A column in *the Interpreter* magazine devotes itself to such sharing, but each issue contains ten times more advice from national experts.

Follow-Up

One final communications need is felt in the church. Lay persons especially express a real need for follow-up information about programs to which funds have been given. A Waynesville, North Carolina, layman said it. "Some kind of message is needed that comes back to our folks saying, Look what your money has done!"

A pastor in Michigan confessed, "I give my people the old 'rathole' treatment. We receive a special offering and never tell them how much is raised or what results from their giving. It just disappears down the old rathole." Unless some message gets back indicating that something good resulted from an offering or a paid-up apportionment, people will not continue to respond with positive feelings.

To Summarize

Fund promotion at its best is faithful to the highest criteria of what constitutes good education. It is focused more on the need for persons to give than it is on the need for institutions to receive. It not only conveys information but inspiration. It emphasizes the vital link between what is happening in ministry and mission and what happens to the individual who seeks to participate in that Christian ministry and mission. It downplays the structure and organization except to portray them as dependable mechanisms for persons to use in their desire to participate in significant Christian work.

A layman from Tulsa put it quite well, "I trust we can educate our people to the real values of the connectional system and let more of our people see what The United Methodist Church is all about—locally, conference wide, and nationally. We have a great church. We are doing great things, and our folks need to be told that over and over again."

CHAPTER 13

Where to Now?

So what about the future? Across the church there is a general optimism about Christianity, The United Methodist Church, and about individual local churches as we move toward our third century. "How can I be anything but optimistic?" asked a Kentucky layman. "It's God's church, isn't it?" A member of Good News commented, "If I wasn't optimistic about the church, I wouldn't bother to criticize. That's the lifeblood of the church—the involvement of people who care enough to criticize." His opposite number, one who was critical of the church for not being socially concerned enough, added that she could not help but be optimistic. "Life's too short for pessimism!" A layman in Georgia said, "Giving will follow the ability of the church to be seen as a viable instrument for human betterment. The kingdom of God on earth must be seen as a positive note. If the church has lost its perception of its own influence, chances are it won't get a very good response from its own people."

Seen As Positive

Non–United Methodists see the denomination in positive terms. A 1979 Harris public opinion poll of non–United Methodist Church attitudes and opinions concerning The United Methodist Church indicated it is perceived positively by society as a whole. They see the denomination as open and receptive to new members from all walks of life. It is perceived as concerned about the spiritual well-being of its members, highly influential regarding the attitudes and beliefs of its members, and concerned about the poor and minorities. The general public views The United Methodist Church as an open and responsive church with a positive image.

Church leaders and others, when asked why they are optimistic, point to the increased willingness of the members to deal with issues and to work with diversity. They believe the connectional style of the denomination lends itself to survival as a minimum and hopefully to a high quality program meanwhile achieving quantitative growth. "We are put together to get things done without losing our voluntary nature" was the assessment of a California laywoman.

Pessimism About World

Conversely, optimism about the nation and the world is not high in the church. The general economy is seen as very uncertain. People are experiencing a growing distrust of institutions and of each other. Many of the persons questioned see the society backing away from a sense of social responsibility for the poor and the powerless.

There is a general feeling at all levels that anything short of a massive depression will not have a significant effect on the general financial program of the church. There may be some increased difficulty in meeting pledges as money gets tight. Churches may experience cash flow problems. However, most promised pledges will eventually be paid. Some general readjustment toward retaining more funds in the local church may result from a continued inflation or the disproportionate increase in heating, utility, and other local costs. However, these rising costs will be offset by a strong desire in the church to retain its connectional and global commitments.

Stewardship Not Increasing

It would be exciting if the evidence indicated a greater sense of stewardship in the future, which could result in a dramatic increase in the money given to the church. However, that does not seem likely. There is no apparent effort to teach stewardship to children or youth at local levels. In fact, this nurture of the church's future may be decreasing. A move to simpler life styles in the use of energy and the earth's resources is not being accepted in any major way by church members. Certainly, money otherwise spent on high standards of living is not likely to flow into the treasuries of the church. The evidence seems to be that United Methodists will continue to give at an annual per capita rate, as they have in the past decade, that is just slightly ahead of the inflation rate.

Maintaining the Local Church

As we move through the 1980s, there will be pressures to devote more dollars to the work and maintenance of the local church. This pressure will not result from a rejection of national and global programs, but from the increasing costs of running a local church. Energy costs will continue to mount. Repair of and additions to buildings with their attendant high costs for borrowing will be an additional problem.

Another pressure comes from clergy who feel that poor pay may not necessarily be a requirement of the job. Pension costs will remain relatively high, as will the desire on the part of clergy to get out of the parsonage system, a move that can be expensive for the local church in the short term. Once again, the membership will have the personal wealth to absorb these additional costs without curtailing outreach and connectional ministries. What they will do will depend on motivation.

Sometime in the 1980s, a need to replace or refurbish existing church buildings will be evident. Buildings constructed following the Second World War or earlier may need extensive renovation or replacement. It well may be that by the middle 1980s additional churches will need to be constructed. These capital expenditures cannot be met by reallocating existing funds. Existing programs already will be straining church income. New money must be generated. Again, barring some economic disaster, the membership will be financially able to give.

Channel for Decisions

As society further constricts the ability of individuals to make decisions about their world and their individual lives, the church will become increasingly attractive as an avenue through which people can find personal involvement in things that matter. This attractiveness will be enhanced if the church moves away from seeking support for the institution through duty, obligation, and guilt and moves toward an image of itself as the serving channel through which Christians freely can choose to participate in meaningful self-fulfilling ministries and mission.

The wide diversity of programs—local, national, and global—and the multiplicity of kinds of programs—from the most evangelical to the most social activist—further enhance the ability of the church to be the place where individuals can find self-fulfillment through participation. Finally, the trustworthiness of the channels, the ability to assure people that the money gets to its intended place with reasonable speed, low administrative costs, and accountability, all are positive attractions to persons who seek ways to involve themselves in their world and its future.

The future will see a greater emphasis on personal involvement and on the need of people to realize personal fulfillment through financial participation. An emphasis on the voluntary nature of the church, rather than its obligatory mandates, will increase these personal feelings and thus the finances. The church must give its members options even to the extent of accepting gracefully their decision *not* to give. The desire and need to participate not only is involved in finances but also in planning and deciding matters of program. However, this circumstance does not call for abdication of dynamic leadership at all levels.

In the recent past, devotion to grass roots participation has created a leadership vacuum—something I believe those in the local churches never intended. They wanted to be heard but not necessarily always heeded. The last several decades have been so devoted to consensus, to listening to individuals at the local levels, and to managing by broadly determined objectives that the church has become devoid of inspired personal leaders. Decisions are made by committees. Some balance must be found to assure that the membership is heard but also given its deserved leadership. The success or failure to achieve this balance will manifest itself most conspicuously in the arenas where decisions are made about money.

The membership will continue to seek a proliferation of channels through which it can give—some worthy and authorized, some questionable and under the counter, some within the church, and many outside of it. The tacit agreement to allow promotion of World Service Specials may see this channel grow with the other program boards developing constituencies equal to that enjoyed by the Advance. Whether this development can be done without the very careful prioritizng and accounting and administrative safeguards practiced in the Advance is doubtful. Community service agencies, colleges, and other institutions cutoff from federal grants will seek to find support through greater direct contact with local churches and annual conferences.

Estate Planning

It is hoped that members will become more aware of the need for individual estate planning and the attractiveness of deferred giving, both as a tax break and as a means to perpetuate their financial involvement in meaningful ministries. This will not be a financial panacea, but annual conferences and church agencies will profit by investing more energy in cultivating this area of potential income.

Channels Needed

The 1980 General Conference ordered that a serious study be made of the funding systems of the church. Included in this is sure to be an examination of the World Service concept—an apportioned fund that gives basic administrative and program financing to the general agencies. The size of this fund usually is determined somewhere between what the agencies need to do their work and what is believed the traffic will bear. The General Conference decides this matter through a recommendation that comes from the General Council on Finance and Administration, a treasurer oriented agency. The very nature of a treasurer's job calls for prudent conservatism. As a result of a conservative approach, the total asked for World Service has given the general agencies in 1980 only 50 percent of the purchasing power they had in 1968.

As the church moves through the 1980s, a World Service Fund apportionment that reflects the real needs of the general agencies to do their work would be a healthier approach. It is important to allow the local churches that want to have strong, efficient national agencies to do their part in supporting them. To challenge the connection to maintain viable, healthy national agencies would seem to be more important than setting as a goal the 100 percent funding of a more conservative target.

The continued pattern of establishing separate apportioned or special day funds, the tacit agreement to encourage World Service Specials, the Advance, the division of funds among programs, funding promotional efforts, and other matters related to fund-raising and spending all deserve careful study and reevaluation. The denomination might be ready to accept challenges to support needed ministries, even where sizable increases in funds are required, if it is presented to them with some guidance as to priorities. The giver's options and choice must be respected. There must be a stated belief in the ability of the church to recognize and meet real program needs, and the financial requirements of these programs must be presented by leaders unafraid to lead.

Tidying Up

Management oriented persons from the local church to the highest councils of the church will continue to try to perfect the organization by advocating single-line giving, stringent controls of what will be given "credit," and equating unquestioned obedience to the system as some kind of proof of faith in God. The members will continue to resist such effort. Pastors trying to tuck everything into the program budget will discover dozens of leaks as people and groups set up their own ways of raising additional money for other things. The same will happen at the annual conference and at national levels.

The answer is not to give up trying to make the system better but to build into the system enough options to provide choices and varieties for a very diverse membership. Also, there should be less paranoia about what feathers do slip out of the pillow—funds given to non-United Methodist channels. Competition for funds is not with such groups. The competition is with a concept of life that does not recognize self-fulfillment in any kind of giving.

Size

There will continue to be debate about the size and shape of the denomination as an institution. During the 1970s, while membership decreased, there was no comparable shrinkage of the supporting structure. For example, just as many bishops were retained. One jurisdiction fought valiantly not to lose one because of fewer members, and another jurisdiction gave serious consideration to exercising its option to add one. Anyone doubtful that bureaucratic, hierarchal, and institutional patterns grow somewhat in inverse ratio to the size of membership need only compare the number of pages in their most recent annual conference journal to the journal of ten years ago when the membership was larger. Rearguard actions are fought to retain every college, committee, fund, office, building, or anything else once started—no matter how unsure the finances or how debatable the ministry. This unwillingness to live in tents as a pilgrim people may eat seriously into existing revenue by requiring institutional maintenance at the expense of new and more creative ministries. It may make an adventuresome membership less willing to invest through the channels of the church in the future to bring about needed change.

Federal Curtailment

If the federal government succeeds in removing itself from a relatively heavy financial investment in the general welfare of the disadvantaged, a challenging, overwhelming ministry will present itself to the church. Who and what will fill the gap? It is unthinkable to the followers of Christ that the poor, the elderly, or any powerless people would be left to the mercies of occasional charity. Where empowerment and help come from may be a matter of debate—but come it must. The chances are the church will not be able to generate enough money to do the task itself. Many believe it should not try.

The historic pattern is that service ministries have been conceived and given birth in the church and then hopefully brought to maturity within the general society. It would be a step backward to receive these ministries back from society. Possibly, the church will face a fivefold task in the 1980s as a result of the federal government's decision not to fund vital services related to the general welfare. One task will be to continue to stimulate a social conscience that refuses to let these vital services die. Second, if unable to change the direction of the federal government, then the church will need to help generate funding and administration of needed services by state, county, and local government units.

Third, since the federal abdication purports to pump investment money into the private sector, the church will need to place before industry and business the responsibility to provide necessary funds for the continuation of social welfare services. It will also need to make sure they do so in ways that are not manipulative or dehumanizing. Actions as stockholders to influence corporations should be encouraged both by agencies in the church and by church members who are stockholders. The work of the Interfaith Center on Corporate Responsibility should be more widely publicized among individual church members.

Fourth, the church will need to step in and organize needed new community institutions, assist these institutions in acquiring organizational, funding, management, and advocacy skills, and continue to advocate needed social change.

Finally, where all else fails, the church will need to convince its membership that knowingly allowing people to suffer and live at levels that are dehumanizing is a sin. The church must be the agency of last resort, supplying services no one else will furnish and challenging its members to provide the finances required to do the task.

Five Factors

In conclusion, this study has led me to see five factors that well may determine the finances of The United Methodist Church as it moves into its third century.

First, there is a need to move away from the philosophy that there are only a limited number of dollars that members will give to the church. One person describes this as "anticipation fatigue." Expecting a negative reaction to increases, the leadership does not ask for them.

Again and again, the membership has responded to need with additional dollars where the need is demonstrated. The Crusade for Christ proved this principle. The building boom in the 1950s and early 1960s proved it too. At local levels, the average congregation will increase its giving 50 percent for capital improvements. Recent responses to hunger and world disasters has demonstrated the willingness to give more. Local churches, annual conferences, and the general church face increased costs for pensions, continued world hunger, the need for church growth, and a multitude of other opportunities for service as we move into our third century. Which will it be—a belief in limited dollars or a belief in unlimited opportunity?

Second, we must reverse the membership decline. There are far better reasons for doing this than to keep from losing money, but that is a good reason too. Earlier, it was demonstrated that in 1979 the church had $180 million less total income than it would have had if it had not had a net decrease of 7 percent in its membership in twelve years.

Membership decline or gain, more than most other factors, will determine the finances of the church in the future.

Third, for a number of reasons discussed earlier, most pastors have a generally negative attitude toward church finances. They tend to underestimate their members' desire and need to participate financially in the mission and ministry of the church. Evidence seems to indicate many pastors are not well prepared to work with stewardship matters or church finances. Other factors move them toward basically negative or counterproductive approaches. If these highly influential persons achieve a more positive attitude, finances will be helped immeasurably.

Fourth, every effort should be made to move away from an approach to finance that stresses the need for the church to receive and toward one that stresses the need of persons to participate. We need to move away from the heavy reliance on duty and obligation and begin stressing opportunity. We must leave behind the image of sacrifice and the resulting concentration on guilt in favor of fulfillment that moves persons toward a sense of triumph.

Fifth, the church is at its best when it is a glorious movement of people who love each other, themselves, and their Lord. This is true as much or more in the arena of funding and finances as it is in any other part of our life together. The emphasis needs to be on the church as a fellowship, rather than as an organization—as a movement, rather than as an institution.

To Summarize

Finances depend much more on intangible feelings and attitudes than they do on logic and rational thought. Even the secular stock market is affected more by faith and hope than it is by facts and reasoned research. Possibly in a day of computer readouts, of high concern for management skills, and of obsession with organization, we tend to forget or even scoff at the human feelings out of which most of us live.

This voluntary group of people called The United Methodist Church seeks a faith much more akin to a community than to a mathematical formula. When it gives money, it resembles a friend more than it does a logician. Funding in the future may depend on our ability to reinsert the reality of the Incarnation that is at the heart of all we do. Abstract issues give guidance, but hearts strangely warmed supply the strength in any gift.

Our funding channels are tried, and they are found true. Our ministries are global, diverse, and creative in their capacity to change systems and lives. Financial energy is transferred swiftly, cheaply, and accountably. All these factors allow us to affirm our financial system as second to none, and they give us ample reason to be optimistic about the financial future of our church.

The final factor will not be in how efficient or how well organized we are, but in how well we are able to fulfill everyone in the process—the giver, the recipient, and all the persons in-between. Can we do it in such a way that all of us know we have freely chosen to be a part of something magnificent, profoundy personal, truly gobal, and marvelously divine? Will our giving help us in our pilgrimage toward personal fulfillment in Christ Jesus? Our ability to recognize our human, emotional need for personal fulfillment and at the same time to build our financial systems to channel this fulfillment's potent energies will help shape our future as we move through the 1980s and into our third century.